THE
HERB
AND
SPICE
COMPANION
A CONNOISSEUR'S GUIDE

by Kathryn Hawkins

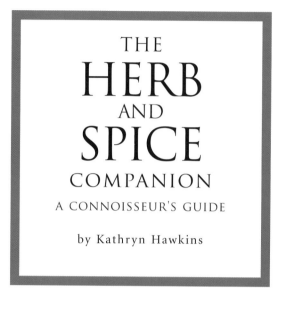

THE
HERB
AND
SPICE
COMPANION
A CONNOISSEUR'S GUIDE

by Kathryn Hawkins

RUNNING PRESS
PHILADELPHIA · LONDON

A Quintet Book

© 2007 Quintet Publishing Ltd

First published in the United States in 2007 by Running Press Book Publishers

Color separation in Singapore by Pica Digital Pte. Ltd.
Printed in China by SNP Leefung Printers Ltd.

9   8   7   6   5   4   3   2   1
Digit on the right indicates the number of this printing

Library of Congress Control Number: 2007920544

ISBN-13: 978-0-7624-3053-6
ISBN-10: 0-7624-3053-2

This book was designed and produced by
Quintet Publishing Limited
6 Blundell Street
London N7 9BH

Designer: Rod Teasdale
Editor: Richard Rosenfeld
Senior Editor: Marian Broderick
Publisher: Gaynor Sermon

This book may be ordered by mail from the publisher.
Please include $2.50 for postage and handling.
But try your bookstore first!

Running Press Book Publishers
2300 Chestnut Street
Philadelphia, PA 19103-4371

Visit us on the web!
www.runningpresscooks.com

CONTENTS

THE WORLD OF HERBS AND SPICES 6

HERB DIRECTORY 8

SPICE DIRECTORY 80

THE WORLD OF
HERBS AND SPICES

Herbs and spices have been enriching our lives for thousands of years. Used for both practical and spiritual purposes, they have been held in high regard since ancient times. In some ancient civilizations, they were worth more than their weight in gold. Today they are so ubiquitous and easily accessible that the world would be a very different place without them.

The powers and uses of herbs and spices are wide ranging. As aromatics, they scent our daily environments and provide us with a touch of luxury. As culinary aids, they produce a huge variety of taste sensations for our comfort and satisfaction. As medicine, they may help provide relief for many ailments. This book offers a general insight into the history and uses of herbs and spices, with particular emphasis on those herbs and spices we value in the kitchen or in food manufacturing.

Classifying what is an herb and what is a spice can be a challenge and, for certain plants, there is some crossover between categories. The origin of the word "herb" comes from the Latin *herba*, which means a grass or green plant. Botanists refer to herbs when referring to a plant with a fleshy stem, but for the purposes of this book, we refer to herbs in the culinary sense: that is, a plant whose green parts (leaves and/or stems) are used to flavor food.

When classifying spice, it is worth taking note of the *Oxford English Dictionary* definition: "One or other of various strongly flavored or aromatic substances from tropical plants, commonly used as condiments."

We should also note that some of the most popular herbs are grown in temperate climates and yield fruit. The fruit, when dried, can often be used as a spice—examples include coriander (cilantro), fennel, and dill. So for the purposes of this book, we refer to the dried parts of a plant: fruit, seed, root, bark, rhizome, and flowers as spices that are used to flavor food. Since dried herbs or spices usually take on a more powerful flavor, it can be said that a spice offers a more intense flavor than an herb.

Over the next few pages, you will discover how herbs have evolved into the flavorings we use today. We aim to give you an insight into how easy it is to grow your own, along with tips on preparing, storing, and using herbs in the kitchen, both fresh and dried. The easy-to-follow herb directory offers information on the most familiar herbs, along with some that are

less well known but are worth investigating. There is a useful description of each herb along with cultivation hints. Finally there are many inspirational recipe suggestions, which will help you expand your culinary repertoire.

In the second half of the book, the spice index continues in the same format. Packed full of historical notes, descriptions, instructions, and suggestions, many familiar spices are included, alongside some of the more unusual ones that you may like to try. Again you'll find a variety of recipes and lots of other suggestions on how to use spices to complement your cooking. Finally, the spice index is followed by popular spice mix recipes, so that you can experiment with your own blends.

This book will become a much-used, much-loved kitchen reference—and next time you're stuck for inspiration to liven up a supper, you'll find an easy solution within its pages. Happy chopping and blending!

Herb
Directory

A Brief History of Herbs

HERBS AS MEDICINE

The ancient Egyptians were among the first to record the use of herbs and flowers pictorially on stone tablets and in tomb paintings. The first written work promoting the use of herbs for health can be dated back to Hippocrates (c.460–370 BC), who compiled a *materia medica* (a book containing information on herbs and their prescription) of more than 400 medicinal herbs.

Hippocrates' works were soon built upon. When the Greek philosopher Aristotle (c.372–287 BC) wrote his monumental 10-volume compendium, *The History of Plants*, it made him one of the most important contributors to our knowledge of botanical science.

In medieval Europe, monks grew herbs for medicinal reasons, using them to treat common ailments and to heal wounds. A monk was the nearest to a physician that ordinary men and women ever met. Thus, in every monastery, a well-stocked and well-tended herb garden was a necessity.

The monks trained each other in treatment procedures and herbal applications. As the information was passed down from generation to generation, many centuries of practice served to support the efficacy of using certain herbal remedies to treat certain illnesses.

The first widely known illustrated book on herbal preparations was written by the English herbalist and surgeon John Gerard. *The Herball, or Generall Historie of Plantes* was published in 1597 and included comprehensive details of each plant, such as origin, history, uses, methods of planting, and the type of soil needed for cultivation.

Jars, sacks, and trays of herbs and spices surround an herbalist at Jacob Mooy and Co. in Amsterdam. The shop was founded in 1743 and is the last of its kind in the Netherlands.

HERBS AND COOKING

From the earliest times, our hunter-gatherer forebears foraged for fruit, nuts, seeds, and herbs, learning by experience what was safe to eat—and which combinations tasted the best.

The first recorded use of herbs for culinary reasons was by the Roman epicure, Apicius. His book featured sophisticated flavoring combinations, such as artichokes cooked with fennel, cilantro, and mint. (Here, too, there may be a medicinal as well as a taste dimension, since some foods, such as artichokes, can be difficult to digest, and some herbs, such as mint, are believed to aid digestion.)

After the fall of the Roman Empire, the influence of Arabian traders spread throughout the Mediterranean. As travelers settled in different regions, they began to grow plants from their homelands, and herbs, such as cilantro, fennel, and mustard, became widely cultivated, surviving even into northerly latitudes.

From the eleventh century, the Crusaders took new ideas and plants from the Holy Lands to Europe, and this started an interest in more exotic herbs and cooking, which grew throughout the medieval period.

One of the uses found for herbs in medieval books was as food colorants. Fresh green herbs, particularly parsley, were used to make ordinary ingredients look more attractive and enticing. During the warmer months of the year, herbs and spices were frequently used to disguise poor-quality ingredients by masking their taste, disguising their color, and giving a touch of much-needed freshness.

Cooking with herbs continued to increase in popularity through the seventeenth century. *Acetaria, A Discourse of Sallets,* written by John Evelyn in 1699, gave a culinary identity to individual herbs. He lists many herbs suitable for cooking and includes details on how they tasted, the parts to be used and how to prepare them, and also information on serving.

From then on, herbs could be viewed as having specific properties and flavors, which could be matched with other ingredients to give delicious combinations.

While many herbs retained their reputation in folk medicine, they were now also seen as foodstuffs—being important for flavor, aroma, presentation, and to make other less interesting

MEASUREMENTS

- All recipe ingredients are given in American customary units.

- Abbreviations used are the following: tsp (teaspoon), tbsp (tablespoon), ml (milliliter), l (liter), g (gram), oz (ounce), fl oz (fluid ounce), kg (kilogram), m (meter), F (Fahrenheit), C (Celsius), in. (inch), ft. (feet). A teaspoon is 5ml and a tablespoon is 15ml.

- All weights are given in pounds or ounces. Approximately $^1/_8$ oz (5g) = approximately 2 tsp; $^1/_4$ oz (10g) = 4 tsp = 20ml; and $1^1/_4$ oz (40g) = 5 tbsp = 80ml.

- For any recipes using eggs, medium-sized eggs are used unless otherwise specified.

- A pinch or dash of spice means the merest pinch or dash—not a handful.

ingredients more palatable. Recipes for specific herb blends were developed for flavoring rich meat casseroles, fish dishes, preserves, relishes, and desserts.

Herbs today

The ease of foreign travel has led to a widespread interest in ever more exotic and original ingredients and flavor combinations. Nowadays we are tantalized by new tastes, smells, and textures, and we are able to import many more exotic herbs than ever before.

On the other hand, the trend toward reducing food air miles has also lead to an increased interest in sourcing food locally. There is a resurgence of interest in old, forgotten varieties, which are widely regarded as having more flavor, color, and texture because they are not commercially mass produced.

Growing your own produce, too, is more popular than ever. Whether you have a garden, an allotment, a few tubs on the patio, or even a windowbox, herbs are among the easiest plants to grow.

GROWING HERBS

Enormous satisfaction can be had from cultivating an herb garden—or even growing just a pot of herbs. They are versatile; although most enjoy a sunny location, there are many that thrive in shady places, such as chives, horseradish, lemon balm, mint, violet, angelica, chervil, and parsley.

Including certain special herbs in your herb garden protects your other plants from pests. For example, if you plant rosemary and/or sage with your other herbs, you will prevent garden pests from destroying crops without needing to resort to chemical agents.

The quality of your soil is crucial when growing herbs. The soils are generally loam-based, tending toward a sandy texture rather than a clay texture. A soil that has the characteristics of strength and lightness is the best medium in which to grow any herbs, irrespective of their species. For your herbs to obtain optimal nutrition from the soil, make sure that the pH is slightly acidic to neutral (pH 6.5-7.9).

Most garden centers will stock a pH testing kit. If your soil is too acidic, add some lime powder and if it is too alkaline, add some sulfur. Similarly check the consistency of your soil: A sticky, muddy soil may need a little sand worked into it, while a stiff clay-based soil will benefit from some peat.

Aspect is an important consideration for all plants, including herbs. Most herbs need at least six hours of sunlight per day, so a south- or southwest-facing aspect is best. However, the patch should also be screened to the north and west by high-growing shrubs, conifers, or a wall, while keeping the south and east aspects of the herb garden exposed.

Water is a vital resource for most herbs, apart from a few drought-tolerant species, such as rosemary. Plant them as close to your water source as possible. They respond well to rainwater, so investing in a water butt to collect this precious resource is a sensible, money-saving idea.

Herbs in the garden

Planning your herb garden is crucial. Ask yourself what herbs you need for cooking. Do you prefer delicate dishes flavored with a touch of parsley or tarragon? Or are you a lover of Mediterranean dishes, more robustly seasoned with basil, rosemary, or oregano? Or do you prefer western Asian cooking with its delicious touches of mint or cilantro?

Grow only the culinary herbs that you use on a regular basis. Check which herbs are always running low in your kitchen, and this will tell you what to grow. As you learn more about growing herbs and become more adventurous, you can always add new plants to your collection.

Large or small garden?

Growing herbs in a large garden will take some planning, and a visit to an established public herb garden will give you valuable ideas to bring home, especially if you are planning on planting a wide variety. An herb border is an attractive addition to a larger garden—but care must be taken not to overplant the area.

In a smaller garden the available space dictates what you can plant in the way of herbs but, with imagination, there are an infinite number of ways to create an impressive herbal display. For those with no garden, planting in containers is a convenient and satisfying way to ensure you have a supply of fresh herbs.

Container herbs

The number of herbs kept in a container depends, of course, on the size of the container—a large half-barrel, for example, could house a mini-herb garden. Whatever your container of choice, herbs in pots need to be watered regularly and given as much sunshine as possible.

Check the growing instructions for all herbs that you plant together. Don't forget that herbs spread out and some grow very fast, so allow plenty of room at the time of planting.

Window boxes planted with herbs make a colorful and decorative display, which livens up any dull wall or ledge. Don't forget to place plenty of crocks in the bottom to aid drainage.

If herbs are planted in a hanging container, be aware that the wind has a dramatic drying effect. When planting up your basket, place a shallow tray in the bottom to create a built-in reservoir for storing water. This benefits your herbs, especially through the hot summer months.

Terra-cotta or glazed pottery containers look stunning when planted, but they must be protected from frost, which may crack them.

USING FRESH HERBS

Fresh herbs require little preparation before cooking but, as they are often quite delicate, care should be taken not to damage them. For robust herbs, such as thyme and rosemary, you can rinse them quite easily in cold running water and then shake them to remove excess water before chopping. For fine-leaved varieties, such as basil, dill, or tarragon, fill a large bowl with cold water and lower the herbs into the bowl in a strainer or colander. Rinse them and then lift out. Shake off the excess water and then carefully pat dry on kitchen paper.

It is important to remember that the art of flavoring in cooking is to use just enough to enhance the dish, not to overpower the final result. In most cases, use at least twice the amount of fresh herb to give the same intensity of flavor as its dried equivalent, but remember that the flavor quality of the dried herb does not compare well with the fresh. Prepare the herbs as close to cooking as possible in order to preserve flavor and color.

Different herbs have an affinity with different foods, which makes cooking with them an exciting and enjoyable activity. Woody textured herbs and those with a resinous flavor such as bay, rosemary, sage, and thyme go best with more robust ingredients like game, red meats, and spicy foods. These herbs will sustain longer cooking and are often added at the beginning of a recipe to allow their flavor to develop gradually. More delicate herbs, such as chervil, dill, and tarragon are best with poultry, seafood, and vegetables. These herbs are usually added chopped toward the end of cooking and left in to give color as well as flavor.

USING DRIED HERBS

For most herbs there is no comparison to that of a freshly picked sprig, but if you wish to keep a supply on hand, the best culinary herbs to dry are thyme, tarragon, bay leaves, and rosemary. These hold their aroma and taste for a good long time, but in general it is not wise to keep dried herbs for more than 12 months since the aroma and flavor reduce dramatically after this period.

When drying the herbs, it is best to collect them just before the buds open—this ensures that the leaves contain the highest concentrations of oils and essential agents. Thyme and tarragon can be tied together and hung in bunches to dry. Flowering herbs, such as lavender and chamomile, can be dried on the stem and are best tied in bunches and hung upside down for drying. For the larger-leaf varieties of herbs, such as mint, basil, and sage, pick only perfect leaves early in the day before the sun has a chance to dry out the essential oils. Once they have been picked, hang the bundles in a warm place to dry out to a point where they are brittle enough to crumble and store in an appropriate container.

Once your herbs are dried, keep them in individual storage bottles or jars that are clearly marked with the name of the herb and the date harvested. The bottles or jars need to be clean, airtight, and kept in a dry, dark place.

HERBS BY COMMON NAME

GARLIC
Allium sativum

*Believed to have originated from Asia, the ancient Egyptians
actually worshipped garlic and fed it to their
slaves to keep them fit and well.*

Garlic has been a staple of Mediterranean cooking for many hundreds of years. A powerful flavoring with antiseptic, antibiotic, and antifungal properties, it is just as at home in the apothecary as in the kitchen.

There are white, pink, and purple varieties of garlic bulb, and each variety's flavors can vary from sweet and mild to very strong. With its pungent and savory taste, which is much stronger than any onion, garlic is not to everyone's taste—yet it is one of the most popular and commonly used herbs in the world.

Description and parts used

Garlic grows as a bulb underground. Above ground there are flat, solid, bright green leaves and white flowers. The bulb is the main part used, but the leaves and flowers can also be included in recipes.

❦ CULINARY USES ❦

Garlic can be eaten green (fresh) or, more commonly, dried. Avoid using a wooden board for chopping or crushing fresh garlic because the wood becomes saturated with the aromatic oils. Green garlic has a delicate, fresh flavor and aroma, and can be used as a replacement for dry garlic, onions, or leeks in any recipe—it doesn't need peeling. The stem gives a delicate flavor to salads and savory juices. Dry garlic needs to be peeled although can be slow-roasted whole and served as an accompaniment for roasted game, poultry, and red meats. Otherwise, peel and chop fine for soups, casseroles, rice, pasta, and vegetable dishes. You can preserve fresh garlic in oil and vinegar and the bulbs can also be dried. Don't freeze because the flavor deteriorates.

CHICKEN WITH 40 CLOVES OF GARLIC

This delicious way to make a special roasted chicken is perfect for
a get-together of garlic-lovers. Serves 4.

INGREDIENTS

3 lb oven-ready chicken
Salt and freshly ground black pepper
1 small bunch each of chervil, tarragon,
  rosemary, and thyme
2 bay leaves
1 large fennel bulb, trimmed
4 tbsp olive oil
40 cloves garlic, unpeeled
1 tbsp fennel seeds
Fresh herbs to garnish

METHOD

1 Preheat the oven to 375°F. Wash and pat dry
  the chicken. Season all over and put a few
  sprigs of each herb and one bay leaf in the
  chicken cavity. Put the chicken in a large, oval
  casserole with a tight-fitting lid.

2 Cut the fennel in thick slices and then cut
  each slice in half. Arrange around the chicken.

3 Mix the oil, garlic, and fennel seeds together,
  and pile over and around the chicken. Tie the
  remaining herbs together and place on top of
  the chicken. Cover the casserole with a layer
  of aluminum foil and then place the lid on top.
  Bake for 90 to 110 minutes, or until the chicken
  juices run clear.

4 Transfer the chicken to a warm serving platter,
  cover with aluminum foil, and stand for
  15 minutes. Discard the herbs and, using a
  draining spoon, remove the fennel and garlic
  from the casserole to arrange around the
  chicken. Garnish the chicken with fresh
  herbs and serve.

CHIVE
Allium schoenoprasum

*The chive is a member of the allium family, which also includes
onions, garlic—and lilies! It was first discovered
more than 5,000 years ago in China.*

For many years, chives have grown wild over most of the Northern Hemisphere, including the harsh conditions of Siberia, Sweden and North America. The Romans took them to western Europe where they thrived, and they are now one of the most common and easily grown garden herbs.

In the past, chives were known as the "Little Brothers of the Onion," because of their mild, oniony flavor. They are high in vitamin C and iron. For this reason they are considered to be a highly nutritious food and excellent for building up the blood. Chives also have a mild stimulant effect on the appetite and can aid digestion.

Description and parts used

This hardy plant grows in bunches like tall grass. It can be quite invasive so it is a good idea to grow the herb in containers. In the kitchen, the long thin tubular leaves and flowers are used.

❦ CULINARY USES ❦

Chives produce a mild onion flavor that is best released by snipping the leaves and adding them to the dish on serving, before the oils can evaporate. Use in salads and soups, where onions would be too strong, and also as a garnish, and in dressings. Try adding chives to vegetables of all kinds, fish, salads, baked potatoes, and egg dishes. As a garnish, chives mix well with chopped parsley for color and a fresh flavor.

Chives dry well but the flavor is milder than fresh chives. Keep picked leaves well sealed in a container or bag in the refrigerator for a few days. Alternatively, for convenience, you can try chopping them and freezing them in an ice cube tray with a little water. You can then add the cube directly to soups, sauces, or casseroles.

LEMON VERBENA
Aloysia triphylla (Lippia citriodora)

*If you brush past this herb in the garden you'll
be greeted by a waft of sharp, lemony
scent that's hard to beat.*

Originating in South America, this herb was taken by Spanish conquistadors to Europe in the seventeenth century. There it gained in popularity as its perfumed oil became widely used in cosmetics and potpourri. Medicinally, lemon verbena in small amounts is said to relieve bronchial congestion, indigestion, stomach cramps, and nausea. In the kitchen, the leaves can be used to impart a sweet lemony fragrance to many dishes, instead of using fresh citrus fruits. The leaves can be harvested at any time but are at their best before the plant flowers.

Description and parts used

Lemon verbena is a tall, spindly plant that grows 2–4 ft. high in a temperate climate. In hot conditions it can reach 15 ft. high! It has long pointed rough-textured leaves with a central vein, which grow off a woody stem. Lemon verbena has tiny white and lilac flower clusters that form in late summer.

❧ CULINARY USES ❧

Infuse in an herb tea to drink hot or allow to cool, then add to a punch for a refreshing citrusy kick, or simply add the leaves to flavor fresh lemonade. Finely chop young leaves and add to flavor fruit desserts, confectionery, preserves, and to sugars for topping cakes and desserts. Add a few sprigs to baking fish dishes to infuse the cooking stock. Lemon verbena can also be left to infuse in water to make a refreshing finger bowl. Sprays of the foliage make a stunning arrangement set in an ice bowl to serve lemon or other citrus sorbets.

Lemon verbena leaves can be dried successfully and stay fresh for many months, if prepared and stored correctly. Try preserving in oil and vinegar to give salad dressings and marinades a touch of citrus.

DILL WEED
Anethum graveolens

The name comes from the old Norse word dilla, *which means
to lull or to soothe, and it has mild sedative properties.
Both the seeds and the leaves of dill can be used.*

Dill water, also known as gripe water, has been used for centuries to soothe colicky and fretful small babies. In medieval times, it was thought to be a magic herb and, as such, was used to combat witchcraft. It was also used in love potions for the same reason.

Dill weed is a native of northern Europe and Russia. It is now cultivated throughout the world, but mainly in the Northern Hemisphere. Dill was taken to North America by early settlers and the seeds became known as "meeting-house seeds" because they were chewed to stave off hunger during long sermons. Dill weed was not grown commercially in North America until the nineteenth century.

Description and parts used

A tall, spindly plant that grows nearly 6¹/₂ ft. tall, with slender stems and aromatic, feathery, threadlike greenish blue leaves. The seeds are also used as a spice (see page 92).

🐝 CULINARY USES 🐝

Dill weed has a slight anise seed flavor and, traditionally, the leaves have been used to flavor pickled cucumbers and gherkins all over Europe, especially in the eastern countries. If you use the leaves in any hot dishes, add them near the end of the cooking time to preserve the flavor. Use the chopped leaves in vegetable dishes (especially good with zucchini, tomatoes, beets, and cabbage), and creamy sauces for fish and egg dishes. Use a feathery sprig as an attractive garnish. Dill weed is a popular herb in Scandinavia where it is a common flavoring for the famous gravalax, a raw salmon dish. The leaves dry or freeze well in the same way that chives do (see page 22) and they make a fragrant oil or vinegar for use in dressing fish and other mild dishes.

ANGELICA
Angelica archangelica

*A native plant of damp meadows and river banks, angelica
is a very lush plant with a pungent sweet scent.
Its leaves dry very successfully.*

Legend says that angelica was a cure for plague, which has secured it a place in traditional herbal medicine as a protector against evil and as a popular cure-all. Medicinally, angelica appears to have a beneficial effect on the circulation of blood and body fluids and is used for the treatment of menstrual cramps, fluid retention, and cystitis. It is also used to treat rheumatism and as a tonic for colds and travel sickness.

Description and parts used
Angelica has thick, hollow stems and large, umbelliferous, glossy, bright green leaves. The plant grows 3–8 ft. in height and can give the garden a tropical feel. Chiefly the bright green stem and leaf are used in the kitchen. It is advisable to cut off the flowerheads as soon as they appear in early summer in order to keep the stems and leaves from yellowing.

❦ CULINARY USES ❦

Angelica has a penetrating flavor. Care is needed since some people may find the taste overpowering. The stems are usually candied (see page 77) and used to decorate cakes and desserts—choose fresh, young, green stems the thickness of pencils for the best results when doing this. Try using the leaves for stewing with acidic fruit to give an alternative sweetness to sugar, and the flavor also goes well in a casserole of fish.

Chopped angelica leaves may be used in salads, hot wine, and fruit drinks. It is also used to flavor gin, vermouth, and the herbal liqueur Chartreuse. In northern Europe and Siberia, the midribs of angelica leaves are cooked and eaten like asparagus, and the roots are dried and added to rye bread.

COMMON CHERVIL
Anthriscus cerefolium

*Often overlooked in the kitchen due to the popularity
of parsley, chervil is an herb well worth
considering as an alternative.*

Chervil has a much more delicate flavor than parsley and is slightly warming when eaten raw. It is very popular in French cuisine, being one of the traditional group of culinary herbs known as *fines herbes*. A native of southeastern Europe and western Asia, today it grows on every continent. Seventeenth-century Dutch settlers introduced it to North America.

Medicinally, raw chervil provides good vitamin C and A, iron and magnesium. Infused as a tea it will help digestion and alleviate circulation disorders.

Description and parts used

Chervil grows in graceful clumps about 10–15 in. high with slender hollow stems and fine feathery fernlike light green leaves. The stems and leaves are used in the kitchen, and as the plants are very delicate, it is best to snip off the leaves with scissors rather than breaking them off.

❦ CULINARY USES ❦

At its best when combined with delicate flavors, such as eggs, chicken, and fish, chervil makes a pretty garnish for cold foods. However, bear in mind that, when you sprinkle it on hot food, it wilts quickly. Use generously in salads and to sprinkle over cooked vegetables, especially carrots. It makes a subtle seasoning for a stuffing for chicken or veal. A sprig can also be added to milk or cream to infuse and give a delicate flavor to desserts, or to make white and cream sauces to go with fish. Add freshly chopped chervil toward the end of cooking time in order to preserve as much flavor as possible. Chervil is used commercially to flavor liqueurs. The leaves are too delicate to dry so they are best frozen (see page 22 for freezing tips). Mix with vinegars to add a subtle flavor.

BURDOCK
Arctium lappa

Once you've started growing all the popular herbs, it's time to focus on the more intriguing, and the highly versatile burdock certainly comes top of the list, perking up stir-fries, and much else.

Commonly found growing by dry roadsides and on wasteland in temperate climates, burdock has a number of variants. The bitter leaves of the wild plant can be steeped in water with dandelion, but the root is more commonly used, to make dandelion and burdock beer. The flavor of burdock is astringently sweet, and the texture sticky. In medicine, burdock is used to temper skin inflammations, control bacterial infections, or as a decoction to cleanse the blood.

Description and parts used

Above ground, burdock's oval dull green, downy leaves can grow quite large, extending to a height of 3 ft. Before the leaves get too big, the young shoots can be picked and eaten in spring. Burdock also has small, purple, nonedible flowerheads in late summer that shed petals, leaving behind clinging burs. The pale thick roots can be lifted in fall, and are the most widely used part in the kitchen.

❧ CULINARY USES ❧

The roots of burdock can be eaten raw—simply wash and peel, then shred and serve as a salad vegetable. They can also be peeled and cooked like carrots or parsnips, and served as a vegetable.

In Japan, the roots are traditionally cut into strips and used in a stir-fry, or are served as part of a delicately flavored salad with other raw roots. Just dress with light soy sauce, toasted sesame seeds, and a little ginger. Peel or scrape the tender leaf stems for braising like celery, or add to soups and broths. Lightly chop the leaf shoots and add sparingly (because they can be quite bitter) to a salad.

The root is best used fresh, although the young leaf shoots can be dried successfully.

FRENCH TARRAGON
Artemisia dracunculus

The name tarragon derives from estragon, *the French word
for dragon, because it was believed that it could cure
the bites of venomous creatures.*

Though it has little scent, French tarragon has a mild pepper flavor with a hint of anise seed. The herb's origins are uncertain, but it probably came from Asia and was first introduced to Europe by the Moors when they conquered Spain, although it didn't reach the rest of Europe until the sixteenth century. Today it is a popular culinary herb, widely used in French cooking as part of a *fines herbes* blend. The leaves are rich in iodine, mineral salts, and vitamin C. In the past, tarragon was used as a treatment for a vitamin deficiency known as scurvy. If chewed raw, it can sweeten the breath, and if infused, it can be used as an appetite stimulant, digestive, and general tonic.

Description and parts used

Tarragon has tall, narrow stems growing to 2–3 ft. high with glossy, long, narrow, green leaves that are used in cooking. The curly, taillike root can be used as a cure for toothache.

🐚 CULINARY USES 🐚

Chop the leaves and use sparingly to give a warm, subtle flavor particularly suitable for fish, chicken, egg dishes, salad dressings, mayonnaise, and cream sauces. It makes a lovely salad herb when mixed with soft leaves and cucumber. Chopped with gherkins and capers, tarragon is the main herbal flavoring of tartare sauce, and also an essential ingredient in a Béarnaise sauce. Mixed with butter and chilled, it is delicious when allowed to melt over steaks, chops, broiled fish, and freshly cooked vegetables. It is particularly good with lamb.

Tarragon makes an excellent flavoring in stuffing for chicken and other poultry, such as turkey. Traditionally the leaves are used to flavor vinegar for dressings and sauce making. They are better frozen than dried.

PAN-FRIED CHICKEN WITH TARRAGON

A simple but delicious supper dish when time is short. Serve with freshly cooked baby potatoes and sweet, tender vegetables. Serves 4.

INGREDIENTS

4 boneless, skinless chicken breasts
A few sprigs fresh tarragon
1 tbsp sweet butter
1 cup white wine
2 shallots, peeled and chopped fine
²/₃ cup heavy cream
2 tbsp chopped fresh tarragon
Salt and freshly ground black pepper

METHOD

1 Wipe the chicken breasts with a paper towel and make several slits in each. Insert a few tarragon leaves in the slits and set aside.

2 Lightly brush or spray a skillet with oil then place on a moderate heat until hot. Add the butter and, when melted, add the chicken and cook for 5 to 6 minutes on each side or until done. Remove from the skillet and set aside.

3 Add the wine and shallots to the skillet and bring to a boil. Boil for 2 minutes, then reduce the heat and stir in the cream. Boil gently for 1 minute or until the sauce has thickened slightly.

4 Stir in the tarragon with seasoning to taste, heat for 1 minute, then serve with the cooked chicken and vegetables.

HORSERADISH
Armoracia rusticana

*Originally cultivated as a medicinal herb, since the late
sixteenth century horseradish has become
very much an herb of the kitchen.*

The Germans and Danish use horseradish in a sauce to accompany fish, while in Britain it has become synonymous with traditional roasted beef and Yorkshire pudding.

Horseradish has a sharp pungency that can clear the sinuses in one bite; its volatile oil is released as the root is shredded, but quickly evaporates and is lost completely when cooked.

The fresh root contains calcium, sodium, magnesium, and vitamin C. The oils of horseradish root have antibiotic qualities that are useful for preserving food and protecting the intestinal tract. It can be taken in a syrup as a treatment for coughs and bronchitis.

Description and parts used

Horseradish is a hardy plant with a long, invasive root with cream-colored flesh. Above ground, thick, round stems sprout into large pointed, bright green oval leaves. These have a powerful aroma when bruised.

❦ CULINARY USES ❦

Horseradish gives off a hot, strong, and pungent aroma rather like mustard. Peel and shred—best done using a food processor as the juices are very pungent—and use immediately in dressings, sauces, and salads. Horseradish sauce or relish is an excellent accompaniment for roasted and smoked meats. Shred into coleslaw and dips, or sprinkle over sliced tomato and pickled beets, or mix with cream cheese, mayonnaise, and mashed avocado for sandwich fillings. Try chopping young leaves and add to salads to serve with smoked fish.

Excess shredded root is best when sealed in freezer bags. It can be frozen for up to six months. Whole washed roots can be preserved in vinegar. Horseradish leaves dry successfully.

CREAMED HORSERADISH RELISH

This piquant sauce is attractive and delicious served with these modern appetizers of roasted beef canapés. Serves 4 to 6.

INGREDIENTS

Scant ¹/₂ cup heavy cream
1¹/₂ oz piece horseradish root
1 tsp Dijon mustard
2 tsp white wine vinegar
1 tsp superfine sugar
1 tbsp fresh thyme, fine chopped
Salt and freshly ground black pepper

METHOD

1 Whip the heavy cream until just peaking. Peel and finely grate or mince the horseradish. Place in a small bowl and mix with the remaining ingredients.

2 Fold the horseradish mixture into the heavy cream. Garnish with some thyme sprigs and serve immediately.

BORAGE
Borago officinalis

Borage is native to Mediterranean areas and was taken to central Europe by the Romans. Early settlers took it to North America where it now grows wild.

A familiar herb to cooks, borage has been considered a mood-enhancer and is associated with inspiring courage. This reputation for "lifting the spirits" dates back to John Gerard, who included it in his famous herbal writings, and claimed that the cucumber-flavored borage could "drive away sorrow and increase the joy of the mind." In fact, borage does contain high amounts of potassium, calcium, and mineral salts. These are stimulating to the adrenal gland, which is the part of the body responsible for the release of adrenaline.

Description and parts used

Borage has a sturdy, round, hollow, branching stem with prickly white hairs. It can grow to 1–2 ft., and has dark green, pointed leaves, also covered with white hairs. The flowers are deep blue (sometimes pink) five-petaled stars with black stamens. Both flower and leaf can be used in the kitchen.

❦ CULINARY USES ❦

To pick the flowerheads, grasp the black stamen tips and gently separate the flower from its green back. These stunning flowers make an attractive garnish. They can be candied (see page 77) and used to decorate sweet dishes, cakes, and desserts. The flowers and chopped young leaves are traditionally added to Pimms No.1 cup for their cooling effect and refreshing flavor. Add chopped young leaves and flowers to vegetable and pasta dishes, or add leaves to salads as a garnish, or sprinkle over cucumber dishes to enhance the flavor. Older leaves can be cooked in the same way as spinach.

The flowers can be dried successfully. When frozen into ice cubes they make a stunning addition to a clear cocktail.

CALENDULA (MARIGOLD)
Calendula officinalis

As well as being a popular and colorful flower in the summer garden, calendula, also known as marigold, is a versatile herb with many uses.

Calendula can be used cosmetically, medicinally, as a dye for cloth, and as a culinary ingredient. The ancient Egyptians worshipped its healing properties—while ancient Persians and Greeks garnished food with it. Modern-day Hindus use the flower to decorate temples and altars. In Europe, calendula is used to flavor soups and casseroles, and to color cheese, butter, and milk dishes. Calendula has soothing, antiseptic qualities and is a popular treatment for cracked skin and chapped lips.

Description and parts used

The green succulent stem covered in fine hairs grows to a height of 12–20 in. The leaves are green in color, slightly hairy, and resemble broad tarragon leaves. The stunning flowers are 2–3 in. wide, with golden yellow-orange petals radiating from a darker center. The petals and leaves are widely used in the kitchen.

❦ CULINARY USES ❦

Add fresh petals to sweet salads for color and distinct flavor, or to make a pretty garnish sprinkled over fish, chicken, and rice dishes, or over a platter of cold meats.

They can be used in place of saffron for color—although they are no substitute for the perfumed flavor—and they provide a light, slightly citrus, tangy, flavor. Try adding to rice, fish, and meat soups, omelets, milk and cream infusions, cakes, and sweet breads. Add 1 teaspoon of calendula petals to a venison casserole for a bittersweet flavor. Chop young leaves finely and toss into salads and casseroles.

Dry the petals at a low temperature in order to preserve their color, or macerate in oil.
Caution: Avoid during pregnancy.

CHAMOMILE
Chamaemelum

Chamomile is the name given to several daisylike plants, but only two are important as herbs: C. nobile *(Roman chamomile) and* C. Matriacaria recutita *(wild or German chamomile).*

Roman chamomile is often grown as a lawn and gives a soothing fragrance when walked upon on a summer's evening. The German variety is preferred for medicinal use, although the Roman variety is also suitable.

The ancient Egyptians make reference to the use of chamomile in their writings. Probably because of its golden flowerheads, they dedicated the herb to the sun and worshipped it above all others for its healing powers. Chamomile is also valued for its sweet apple-scented leaves, bitter and aromatic in flavor, and has been taken for centuries as a tea to calm the nerves and induce rest.

Description and parts used

Tall thin rounded stems that grow to about 4–12 in. The leaves are apple-scented, bright green, and finely cut. The scented flowers have a large, domed, golden yellow center with white petals.

❦ CULINARY USES ❦

The flowers are dried and used as a tea for a general tonic or sedative—try adding cold chamomile tea to apple juice punches and smoothies, or make a sugar syrup and infuse with the flowers as a base for cordials. Chamomile goes well with the flavor of apples and pears, so use the cold herb tea or cordial to make up a jelly or creamy mold. In Spain, the bitter flowers are used to flavor Manzanilla sherry, which is served at the beginning of a meal as an aperitif. Chamomile is also added to herb beers.

Dry the flowers and leaves in bunches for making teas and flavorings, and simply crumble into the cup before pouring over hot water. It can also assist digestion and soothe an upset stomach, and it has antiseptic properties. Do not freeze.

CHICORY
Cichorium intybus

Grown as a vegetable and used as a tonic by the Romans, chicory remains
an important cultivated crop in Europe. The roots
and leaves have different uses.

There are three main varieties of chicory, but the most common is Witloof, or Belgian chicory. It has a compact elongated head called a chicon, which can be served either cooked as a vegetable, or raw as a bitter salad leaf. The roots are roasted and mixed with coffee (especially in France). The young roots have a slightly bitter, caramel flavor, and older roots are very bitter. In medicine, the dried root is used in a tonic with mild laxative and diuretic effects. It is also used to soothe inflammation of the kidneys and urinary system.

Description and parts used

The long, thick, and fleshy taproot, sometimes branching, has bitter, milky fluid inside when cut, and can be dug in the fall of the first year of planting. The young mid-green arrow-shaped, dog-toothed leaves and bright blue dandelionlike flowers can also be eaten. If grown in acid soil, the flowers will be red.

🌑 CULINARY USES 🌑

Scrub and wash young chicory roots, boil as root vegetables, and serve with a lightly seasoned, creamy sauce. For a coffee substitute, use the thicker roots. Wash them, slice and dry at a low heat, then roast and grind as you would coffee beans.

Young juicy leaves can be eaten as a salad leaf (they have a dandelion flavor) or sautéed in butter like spinach. The flower buds can be pickled in vinegar and used in salads with cold meats and oily fish. Fresh blooms make a stunning addition to a bowl of leaves or used as a garnish for smoked or oily fish.

Dry the root and leaves to preserve. Preserve flower buds in vinegar. The flower petals are often dried and added to potpourri.

CILANTRO (CORIANDER)
Coriandrum sativum

*Cilantro has been used as a culinary and medicinal herb
for at least 3,000 years. It is a native of southern Europe,
northern Africa and central Asia.*

Cilantro was taken to Europe by the Romans who mixed it with cumin and vinegar, and used it as a meat preservative. All parts of the plant are edible, all having a pungent aroma, but the dried seeds have a real sweetness (see page 111). Today, cilantro is widely used all over the world, especially in Thai, Indian, and Middle Eastern cooking and it is one of the most popular and important culinary herbs in the twenty-first century.

Medicinally, it can be chewed or made into a tea to aid digestion and to stimulate the appetite. It also reduces flatulence and helps relieve colic.

Description and parts used

A delicate plant that likes full sun, cilantro grows to a height of 2 ft. The stems are fine, rounded, branchlike and pale green. The leaves are soft, broad, and finely scalloped. The leaves and seeds are commonly used.

❦ CULINARY USES ❦

Prepare coriander leaves just before using. They are best cooked lightly or not at all—merely stir them in at the end of cooking or sprinkle on top of a finished dish. Use fresh chopped coriander leaves sprinkled over poultry, rich casseroles, soups, and curries. Add a handful of young leaves to green salads and chop into salad dressings and mayonnaise. Sprays of coriander make an attractive garnish. The roots can be cleaned and ground to make a paste for curries (see page 155.)

The leaves don't dry well but, if picked with the root, they will keep in a pitcher of water in the refrigerator for several days; cover the top with a plastic bag to retain flavor and freshness. The leaves will freeze in ice cubes in the same way as chives (see page 22).

TOMATO AND CILANTRO SOUP

The citrus-like flavor of the cilantro in this refreshing summer first course perfectly complements the fruit juices in the soup. Serves 6.

INGREDIENTS

3 lb ripe, plump tomatoes, roughly chopped
1 small onion, chopped
³/₄ cup tomato juice
3 tbsp freshly squeezed orange juice
1 red bell pepper, deseeded
³/₄ tsp superfine sugar
Iced water
4 tbsp chopped fresh cilantro
³/₄ cup plain yogurt for garnish

METHOD

1 In a blender purée the tomatoes, onions, tomato juice, orange juice, bell pepper, and sugar.
2 Press the purée through a strainer, rubbing with a wooden spoon to force as much through as possible. Discard the residue, and add sufficient iced water to thin the purée to a souplike consistency.
3 Stir in the cilantro, cover, and chill. Pass the yogurt at the table, to allow guests to add as they wish.

ARUGULA
Eruca vesicaria (E. sativa)

*Once used only as a medicine for the treatment of coughs
and aiding digestion, salad arugula is now used chiefly as
a culinary salad herb—and a trendy one at that!*

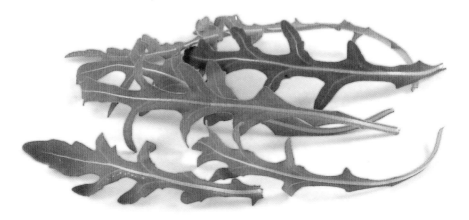

The Romans prized the leaf and seed for its pungent, spicy flavor—it certainly packs a punch on the taste buds even today. Try fresh arugula in the salad bowl or piled on top of pizzas, risottos, or broiled steaks as a tasty, stylish garnish.

Arugula is easy to grow and can sometimes be found growing wild on wasteland.

Description and parts used

The cultivated variety grows to a height of 2–3 ft. and has small cream-yellow flowers that appear in early summer. The leaves are pointed, lance-shaped, and deeply indented near the base of the plant. When the leaves are freshly picked, you quickly notice their peppery fragrance. Make sure you pick them before the plant flowers to ensure that the leaves are of maximum tenderness and minimum pungency. The flowers and seeds can also be used as salad ingredients.

❧ CULINARY USES ❧

In southern France, arugula is part of a much-loved salad of small leaves known as *mesclun*. The leaves are best eaten raw in salads, but can withstand a little cooking, so can be added at the last minute to stir-fries, pasta sauces, and risottos. Alternatively they can be steamed as a vegetable and served in the same way as spinach. Piled high on many finished dishes, arugula looks impressive and attractive. You can also replace the basil in the classic pesto sauce with freshly picked arugula leaves. (For how to make basil pesto sauce, see page 55.)

Once picked, arugula is best eaten immediately because it wilts quickly. The leaves stay fresh if sealed in a container in the refrigerator for 2–3 days, but they are not suitable for freezing or drying.

A SIMPLE ARUGULA SALAD

Ratchet up the style factor of your dinner parties by serving a crisp arugula salad. This salad is good as an accompaniment to everything from pasta to fish to roasted meats. Serves 4.

INGREDIENTS

4 handfuls fresh arugula leaves
12 ripe vine cherry tomatoes, halved
4 scallions, sliced
4 sprigs of fresh basil
Balsamic vinegar and good quality olive oil
  to drizzle
Fresh ground black pepper

METHOD

1 Carefully rinse the arugula leaves in a strainer or colander lowered into a bowl of cold water. Shake off the excess water and pat dry using kitchen paper.
2 Pile on to four serving plates and top with the tomato halves, sliced scallions, and sprigs of basil.
3 To serve, drizzle with balsamic vinegar and olive oil to taste, and grind over black pepper. This salad is delicious served with warm, crusty ciabatta, but to make more of a main meal, add sliced smoked salmon, wafer thin ham, or smoked chicken—or avocado for a vegetarian version.

FENNEL
Foeniculum vulgare

One of the oldest cultivated plants, fennel is native to the Mediterranean. It was highly regarded by Roman gladiators who put it in wreaths around their heads for strength and who ate it for good health.

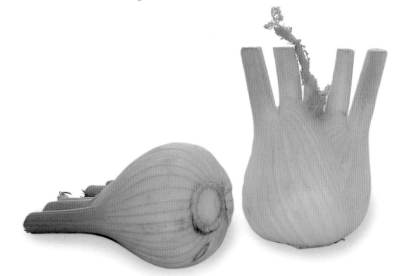

There are two types of fennel available commercially, the green-leaved and the bronze-leaved, both of which have the same fragrant scent and sweet anise seed flavor. Although more concentrated in flavor than dill weed, it can be used in the same way (see page 24). Taken internally as a tea, fennel aids the digestive process and soothes cases of colic and abdominal discomfort.

Description and parts used

If let alone in a flowerbed, the plant can grow up to 7 ft. tall. It has round, shiny green-blue stems with dill-like, lime-green, finely cut leaves that darken in shade as the plant ages. The whole plant is edible from the fine roots to the bulbous root stock eaten as a vegetable, up the stems to the frondlike leaves, and finally the yellow flowerheads, which contain the seeds. Fennel seeds are dried and used as a spice (see page 125).

❦ CULINARY USES ❦

For centuries, fennel has been regarded as one of the main herbs for fish, partly for flavor, but also because it helps counteract the richness of oily fish. Finely chop the leaves and use sprinkled over any salad for a sweet, anise seed flavor, or sprinkle over soups or freshly cooked vegetables to add a freshness and slight zestiness—it livens up bland vegetables, such as turnips, if sprinkled over just before serving. Fennel also goes with lamb, pork, and chicken, and makes a good ingredient in a stuffing or sauce for these foods. The leaves also make a good flavoring for oils and vinegars.

Chopped fennel leaves don't dry well, but you can freeze them in the same way as for chives (see page 22). **Caution: Avoid during pregnancy.**

EGGPLANT, FENNEL, AND WALNUT SALAD

The salted walnuts really bring this salad to life, and complement
eggplant and fennel well. Serves 6.

INGREDIENTS

3/4 cup olive oil

1 fennel bulb, finely sliced, feather leaves reserved
for garnish

1 small red onion, sliced

3/4 cup walnut pieces

Salt and freshly ground black pepper

1 large eggplant, cut into 1/2-inch pieces

1 tbsp red wine vinegar

1 tomato, skinned, seeded, and chopped

1 tbsp torn fresh basil leaves

METHOD

1 Heat 3 tablespoons of olive oil in a skillet and
add the fennel and onion. Cook until just soft
but not browned, about 5 to 8 minutes. Remove
with a slotted spoon and place in a salad bowl.

2 Add 2 tablespoons of oil to the skillet, then
stir in the walnut pieces and fry them for
2 minutes, until crisp and browned but not
burned. Remove the nuts from the skillet with
a slotted spoon and drain on paper towels.
Sprinkle with salt and toss the nuts until coated
and cool.

3 Add 4 tablespoons of oil to the skillet, then add
the eggplant and fry over a moderate heat until
tender and browned on all sides. Remove from
the skillet and add to the fennel and onion.

4 Add the remaining oil to the skillet with the red
wine vinegar and season. Heat until simmering,
then pour over the vegetables in the bowl.

5 While still slightly warm, add the salted
walnuts, chopped tomato, and basil. Allow to
cool, then serve garnished with fennel leaves.

SWEET WOODRUFF
Galium odoratum

Sweet woodruff is a small delicate herb from yesteryear.
Its pleasant aroma is similar to vanilla when fresh, and
reminiscent of new-mown hay when dried.

In days gone by, garlands of sweet woodruff were hung in churches, sprinkled in potpourri, and used throughout the household to give a cheery fragrant atmosphere. It grows wild all over Europe, Scandinavia, in parts of Asia, and in the US, apart from the extreme southern states. It has been used in the kitchen and as a medicine since the medieval period. Dried leaves are infused in a tea to calm the nerves and to aid relaxation.

Description and parts used

Sweet woodruff grows on the outskirts of wooded areas and likes partial shade—it is particularly suited to growing at the base of trees. The bushy plants grow to about 12 in. high. The stems are thin and smooth and the leaves shiny green and arranged in circular spokes that give the plant the second part of its name. In late spring the plant flowers in clusters of bright white star-shaped flowers.

🌰 CULINARY USES 🌰

Sweet woodruff is used to flavor drinks. In Germany, it is combined with Rhine wine and used as a punch for traditional spring festivities. The Swiss use it in a punch with Benedictine, cognac, hock, and vodka, while the French steep it in champagne.

Add sprigs of sweet woodruff to any fruit cup. It imparts a slight vanilla flavor to freshly pressed apple juice, and a touch of sweetness when added to green tea as it brews. Sprigs can also be used to infuse vanilla pie-fillings, sweet cream sauces, and ice cream, or wherever a vanilla pod is used. This herb is best used fresh for the vanilla scent. If you prefer the sweet-hay scent, pick the leaves and flowering stems, and dry them whole. The herb is not suitable for freezing.

CURRY PLANT
Helichrysum italicum

*A sub-shrub from southern Europe, which is a relative newcomer to herbal lists,
and has grown in popularity with the rise in interest in Indian food.
Good for lovers of Far Eastern and Asian food.*

The curry plant is an attractive herb, similar in appearance to lavender, and it is extremely popular with gardeners for its scent and its evergreen, silver foliage.

The leaves have a wonderful sweet aroma similar to mild curry powder. If you brush past the plant, it gives off an aroma so delicious that you may be convinced that someone is enjoying an Indian meal nearby. Like most scents from plants, this effect is heightened after rain. It is an ideal choice for planting in borders.

Description and parts used

Growing to about 18 in. high, the stem is woody near the root base, but where the leaves appear it becomes narrower, paler, and downy. The leaves are long, needlelike, and silver-gray with a sweetish curry aroma. The plant has nonedible, small, yellow flowers.

❧ CULINARY USES ❧

Use curry plant leaves in dishes where only a hint of curry flavor is required, and where the color of curry spices is not required. Add to the cooking water of rice, or add to prepared pickling vinegar to penetrate slowly the preserved vegetables. Also add to boiling root vegetables such as parsnips or carrots— it adds a delicious, mild flavor to soups if you keep the cooking water and use as a broth. Always remove the sprig and leaves before serving because the stem is too woody to eat.

The leaves are best picked and used fresh, but they can be dried. The aroma is lost on freezing. The yellow flowerheads retain their color and can be used for potpourri and flower arrangements.

HYSSOP
Hyssopus officinalis

*For anyone interested in growing a medicinal herb garden, hyssop comes near
the top of the list for its extraordinary range of cures. It's also
a valuable—and highly underrated—kitchen ingredient.*

Hyssop is mentioned in the New Testament for its purification properties, and the name derives from the Hebrew *ezob*, which means "healing herb." These powers come from the high content of camphoraceous oils, and also the discovery that the mold that produces penicillin grows on its leaf. It is effective in treating lung infections, such as bronchitis. It can also be used to relieve coughs and colds and can be added to a gargle for sore throats. In the kitchen, it is used as an aid to the digestion of fatty meat and fish. It has a slightly minty, bitter taste.

Description and parts used

Different varieties of this sub-shrub can grow from 1¹/₂–4 ft. tall. The stems are squarish, branching, and green, and the aromatic leaves are long, narrow, slightly hairy, pointed, and dark green. The edible flowers vary in color (see page 77).

❦ CULINARY USES ❦

Use leaves in small amounts because the flavor can be quite astringent. Rub on the skin of fatty meats, such as goose or pork before cooking. Try adding a few leaves to rich meat dishes including beef or game casseroles, or liver pâtés. It is also ideal for adding to bean- and pulse-based dishes to help with digestion, and it goes well with oily fish for the same reason.

For something a bit different, add a few leaves to the syrup of a citrus fruit salad or fruit cocktail appetizer. Also try adding a pinch of chopped leaves to a plum, peach, or apricot pie, or use as a flavoring for cranberry sauce. Discard the leaves before serving. The young leaves and flowers dry well but are not suitable for freezing. **Caution: Avoid during pregnancy.**

ELECAMPANE
Inula helenium

A highly unusual, but incredibly valuable part of the vegetable garden, elecampane is a large plant that grows wild in damp meadows and roadsides throughout temperate climes in Europe and Asia.

Helen of Troy was said to be gathering this herbal root when she was captured by Paris, hence the second part of the Latin name. The Romans ate the root candied to help digestion, and in the medieval period the roots were sold as pink, flat tablets to alleviate indigestion and asthma, and act as a breath freshener. The root is bitter, pungent, and aromatic, and is used to reduce inflammation and fight bacterial and fungal infections. It stimulates the immune and digestive systems. Its camphor-scented oil is used in the perfume industry.

Description and parts used

The thick, dark brown root is tuberous and its flesh is creamy, smelling of bananas. It is harvested and dried in the fall of the plant's second year, and takes on the aroma of sweet violets. Long, pointed leaves grow to 18 in., with shaggy, yellow, daisylike flowers that can be dried and used in potpourri.

❦ CULINARY USES ❦

When chewed the root has a powerful, warming, bitter flavor, and it was used in Roman cooking to make sauces. It was also eaten salted as an hors d'oeuvre, and at the end of a meal as a digestive. The root can be eaten cooked as a root vegetable, and served with rich meat and other fatty ingredients to counteract the richness and aid digestion.

The root was once used to flavor desserts and fish sauce, though now it is more commonly candied (see page 77) or made into a sweet syrup; when candied it can be sucked as a cough lozenge. It is also used to flavor the liqueur absinthe, and can be steeped in wine to make an uplifting cordial. The root can be sliced and dried, or preserved in sugar syrup.

SWEET BAY
Laurus nobilis

Bay has a shapely presence when grown as a topiarized ball on a single trunk, but if you have low rainfall and free-draining soil it can also be grown as a thick, evergreen hedge providing privacy and an amazing supply of herbs.

The evergreen bay tree grows wild in southern Spain, Morocco, and around the eastern Mediterranean. The Romans held bay in high regard and saw it as a symbol of wisdom and glory, turning it into wreaths of excellence for poets and athletes. The Latin name means "renowned laurel." Bay also aids digestion when taken as an infusion, and is often used as an appetite stimulant.

Description and parts used

An evergreen tree that can grow up to 23 ft. tall. The stems are rich brown, solid, and round. Bay can also be grown in small pots and containers, and is often grown as a single trunk topped by a topiarized ball of leaves. It likes full sun, good drainage, and needs shelter from the wind. The dark green leaves are fragrant, leathery and pointed. The flavor is bitter and woody. Only the leaves from the sweet bay are edible. All other laurels are poisonous.

❦ CULINARY USES ❦

Fresh or dry bay leaves should be added at the start of cooking. They deliver a strong, spicy flavor to broths, soups, and stews. Bay can be added to all meat dishes, and to the poaching water for fish. For sweet dishes, infuse milk and cream with a leaf and use in desserts and vanilla pie-fillings, or add to stewing or baking fruit. Always discard bay leaves before serving. Bay leaves form an essential part of a bouquet garni (see page 152). Added to a jar of dry rice, a bay leaf will add a little fragrance.

The leaves dry well, but use quickly because they soon lose their pungency. Otherwise use fresh, picking the leaves at any time of year. Added to oil or vinegar with other herbs and spices, bay adds a woody note.

SAN FRANCISCO CIOPPINO

If San Francisco has a signature dish, it is cioppino, a wonderful seafood stew.
The broth is rich tomato, which includes wine and herbs. Serves 10 to 12.

INGREDIENTS

¹/₂ cup plus 2 tbsp olive oil

1 large onion, chopped

3 leeks, white part only, chopped

1 red and 1 green bell pepper, chopped

8 garlic cloves, minced

1¹/₂ lb fresh tomatoes, peeled, deseeded, and
chopped, or three 15-oz cans whole tomatoes,
chopped

4 tbsp chopped parsley

2 tsp dried basil

1 tsp dried oregano

¹/₂ tsp dried thyme

2 bay leaves

¹/₄ tsp dried red pepper flakes, or more to taste

2 cups dry red wine

9 cups fish broth

Salt to taste

2 large crabs, cooked and cracked

2 dozen clams in their shells, scrubbed

2 dozen mussels in their shells, scrubbed

1 lb sea bass, swordfish, or other sturdy, non-
oily fish, cut into 1-in cubes

1¹/₂ lb shrimp, shelled, and deveined

METHOD

1 In a very large pan or stockpot, heat ¹/₂ cup
olive oil. Add the onion, leeks, and peppers.
Sauté for 10 minutes.

2 Meanwhile, heat the remaining 2 tablespoons
olive oil in a small sauté pan. Add the garlic
and sauté for 2 minutes. Add the garlic and oil
to the stockpot.

3 Add the tomatoes, herbs, pepper flakes, wine,
and fish broth to the pan. Bring the soup to a
boil, then lower the heat and allow to simmer,
uncovered, for 45 minutes. Taste, adding more
red pepper flakes if a spicier broth is desired,
and add salt if needed.

4 Add the seafood to the broth in stages. First,
add the crab 15 minutes before serving. Then
add the mussels and clams about 10 minutes
before serving. Then add the fish 7 to 8
minutes before serving and, finally, add the
shrimp 3 minutes before serving.

5 Discard the bay leaves and any mussels or
clams whose shells have failed to open. Put the
seafood in each bowl, making sure everyone
gets a selection, ladle over the broth, and serve.

LAVENDER
Lavandula angustifolia (L. officinalis, L. spica)

*Given free-draining ground and a sunny site, you can grow
great swathes of lavender, which can be used to flavor food
and create your own deliciously scented perfumes.*

Lavender was an essential part of the early monastic and medicinal herb garden. The aromatic, sweet smell is unmistakable, and it is said to have antidepressant and mood-elevating effects. Its long-lasting fragrance makes it popular with the perfume industry. Lavender also exhibits powerful sedative and calming properties, and is used for the treatment of digestive problems, anxiety, insomnia, and tension headaches and migraines. Lavender is one of the most popular essential oils for relaxation. *L. angustifolia* is probably the most commonly used kind.

Description and parts used
The long green stem grows from 1½-3 ft., and is topped by small, scented, lilac-blue flower spikes 2-6 in. long. The narrow fragrant leaves are gray-green, and have a bitter taste. They are traditionally used in southern European cooking.

❦ CULINARY USES ❦

The flower buds are usually dried, just before they bloom, and are then ground and used as a flavoring. Fresh flowers can be candied for decorations. Try flavoring preserves with lavender, or adding to cake and cookie mixes. Ice cream and sorbets have a deliciously flowery taste if flavored with the herb. Lavender also goes well with lamb—try adding a few sprigs with rosemary to a roasting joint or to barbecuing meat for a sweet, flowery, woody aroma.

Add the dried buds to coarse salt with dried rosemary, crushed black pepper, and a little sugar as a rub for meat before broiling or barbecuing. Dry the flowering stems by laying on open trays or hanging in small bunches. Add a few stems to vinegar to make a sweetly scented dressing.

LOVAGE
Levisticum officinale

A highly underrated, essential part of any herb garden, lovage has a celery-like taste, and can be used in a huge range of recipes from soups to salads.

Largely neglected since the nineteenth century, lovage has a robust flavor and handsome foliage. It is a native of the Mediterranean, but now grows wild in most of Europe, except Britain. It was used in both kitchen and medicinal gardens in the medieval period, and was considered one of the essential herbs. Taken as an infusion, it can reduce water retention. The seeds are added to liqueurs and cordials, and are chewed to sweeten the breath.

Description and parts used

Growing to a height of 7 ft., the green stems are tall, hollow, rounded, and branching near the top. The leaves are large and aromatic, divided and glossy dark green, and resemble the foliage of flat-leaved parsley. The leaves and stalks are chiefly used in the kitchen, but the roots can be peeled, cooked, and pickled, and the crushed seeds are added to breads and pastries as seasoning.

❦ CULINARY USES ❦

Strong-tasting lovage is best used cautiously. The yeasty, celery flavor can pep up soups, casseroles, and cheese dishes, and even replace a bouillon cube. Rub the leaves into chicken before cooking, or rub the inside of a salad bowl to season the ingredients. Young leaves can be added to a mix of salad leaves and herbs, or added to a dressing to serve with a simple green salad. Made into a tea, lovage makes a rich, savory, hot drink. In New England, the leaves and stems are cooked as a vegetable—simply steam like asparagus and serve with a white sauce.

Drying lovage leaves increases the intensity of the flavor, so use the herb sparingly. The chopped leaves and stems also freeze well (see Chives, page 22). **Caution: Avoid during pregnancy.**

MINT
Mentha

Easily grown and quick to spread, a huge range of mints are now available.
Find a specialist nursery with a wide selection, and choose
according to leaf color and scent.

Originating from the Mediterranean, mint has been highly valued since ancient times. The Greeks and Romans used mint in crowns and table decorations, and to flavor wines and sauces. The Romans traveled with the herb, as did the Pilgrim Fathers who took mint to North America where it is still grown on a large scale. There are hundreds of varieties, all having a refreshing, cooling flavor and aromatic fragrance. Mint is widely used as a treatment for respiratory ailments and indigestion.

Description and parts used

Mint is easy to grow either in sun or in partial shade. An invasive herb, it needs to be well controlled by, for example, growing it in a container. Popular varieties include: applemint (*M. sauveolens*), Moroccan spearmint (*M. spicata*), peppermint (*M. x piperita*), and red raripila mint (*M. raripila rubra*).

❦ CULINARY USES ❦

Use sparingly because mint can quickly overpower other ingredients. Add the leaves to iced tea and punches for a refreshing drink. Freshly chopped leaves are great added to a fruit salad, desserts, and jellies, and mint also goes very well with chocolate. Stirred into yogurt it makes a refreshing dressing for salads and meats (particularly lamb), curries, or as a dip for raw vegetables.

Add sprigs to the water when boiling new potatoes, peas, broad beans, and baby carrots. Sprigs of mint are popular garnishes for many dishes, and small sprigs of leaves are often used to decorate desserts. They look pretty when dusted with superfine sugar. Dry, freeze, or infuse the leaves in vinegar to preserve them.

APPLE, MINT, AND CRANBERRY COOLER

Herbal drinks are wonderfully refreshing—if you love the taste of this classic, try making it double strength! Serves 4.

INGREDIENTS
4 tbsp dried cranberries
2 sprigs fresh mint
1 apple, peeled and sliced
2 cups freshly boiled water

METHOD
1 Put all the ingredients in a large pitcher and pour over the water. Allow to stand for 1 hour. Strain and chill before pouring over ice.

2 To make an alcoholic drink, use 1¹/₂ tablespoons grenadine and 1 measure (1¹/₂ tablespoons) of either gin or vodka per glass.

BERGAMOT
Monarda didyma

A beautiful plant (also known as bee balm) with superb bright scarlet or pink flowers, it livens up any garden.

The species name is believed to derive from its citrus-like scent that is reminiscent of the small, bitter, Italian bergamot orange. A native North American plant drunk by Oswego Indians as a tea, it became a popular drink in New England after the Boston Tea Party in 1773. As a tea it is used to treat nasal congestion and to relieve nausea.

Description and parts used
Tall, hairy stems grow to 2–3 ft. tall with dark green, red-veined leaves, and sweet-tasting, scarlet-pink flowers.

❦ CULINARY USES ❦
Use sparingly in cooking or the taste will dominate. Use to flavor punches, lemonade, preserves, and milk infusions. Add to salads and stuffings for chicken.

SWEET CICELY
Myrrhis odorata

This perennial carries star-shaped white flowers at the start of summer, and thrives in dappled shade.

Sweet cicely has pale green, lacy leaves that carry a woodland scent with an exotic dash of myrrh. It is native to northern Europe and grows all over Britain and North America. The leaves are sweet with a mild anise seed flavor, and are a useful ingredient for those on a sugar-restricted diet.

Description and parts used
A hollow, downy stem with branching, fernlike leaves, it can grow to a height of 3 ft.. The leaves are used in the kitchen but the roots can be peeled and eaten raw or cooked.

❦ CULINARY USES ❦
Stir chopped leaves into salad dressings, egg dishes, vegetable soups, and casseroles, and add to the cooking water for cabbage to inject a hint of sweetness.

MYRTLE
Myrtus communis

A bushy Mediterranean shrub, myrtle comes with a long list of classical allusions. It rarely gets a mention in cookbooks, but can certainly perk up a wide range of recipes.

Myrtle grows wild in southern Europe, North Africa, and the Middle East. The flower is associated with Aphrodite, goddess of love. The Romans used myrtle to decorate the tables at wedding feasts and myrtle is still woven into bridal flowers in the Middle East today. The glossy green leaves are highly aromatic, offering a sweet, spicy orange scent in cooking, and the oil is used in perfumes. Medicinally, myrtle contains powerful antiseptic, astringent, and decongestant elements.

Description and parts used

Myrtle is a half-hardy, evergreen shrub that grows from 8–10 ft. tall; it likes the sun and a sheltered position to protect it against the worst of the winter weather. The stems are aromatic, woody, and red-brown in color. The leaves are shiny, leathery, and dark green with a central crease for flowers. The plant produces edible black berries with a blue bloom.

❦ CULINARY USES ❦

For thousands of years, myrtle leaves and berries have been used in the kitchen. Small branches of myrtle can be laid under roasting meats, such as pork or chicken, laid on hot coals, or laid on top of barbecuing meat to add a spicy, aromatic flavor. Chop the leaves and add to stuffing for pork and game. The leaves can be used to flavor wines and spirits, and can be added to a sugar syrup to infuse it with a citrus flavor.

The berry fruits can be dried and ground like juniper berries—they are widely used in the Middle East where they are known as *mursins*. You can dry the flowers, buds, berries, and leaves. Fresh leaves can be picked year-round and can be infused in vinegar to make a spicy, citrus dressing.

SWEET BASIL
Ocimum basilicum

Basil is one of the best kitchen herbs, and is incredibly easy to grow from seed. Different varieties include the traditional large-leaved Italian type and the small-leaved Asian type, which is ideal for stir-fries.

A sun-loving plant from India, and grown in Asia and Africa for more than 4,000 years, basil is even mentioned in the Bible, as an herb that was growing around Christ's tomb after the resurrection. In sixteenth-century Europe, it was used for medicinal purposes only, but by the seventeenth century had also become common as a culinary herb.

Today it is the sweet (or common) basil that is most widely used in the kitchen. Medicinally, basil has been taken internally for chills, colds and flu, and to ease digestion.

Description and parts used

Usually grown in pots, sweet basil plants will grow to about 18 in. high. They need a spot in full sun and frequent watering. The stem is quite soft, pale green, squarish, and branching. The leaves of sweet basil are oval with a warm, spicy aroma. Both the leaves and stalks are used in the kitchen.

❧ CULINARY USES ❧

Pound basil leaves with oil or tear and add to dishes, but never chop. The leaves are especially good with sweet ripe tomatoes and roasted bell peppers. Basil forms the basis of Italian pesto sauce and of many stuffings for meat. It also goes well with cheese and cured ham. Its pepperiness is surprisingly good with dark bitter chocolate.

Basil can be dried and takes on a sweet, minty taste, but the flavor can't compare with a fresh leaf. To freeze basil, paint the leaves on both sides with olive oil and freeze on waxed paper before packing into sealed containers. Store whole leaves in olive oil with salt, or dry-pack with salt in non-corrosive containers. The leaves also infuse well in vinegar to give a fragrant dressing for salads.

PESTO SAUCE

Basil leaves are the base ingredient of the Italian sauce, pesto, which here
acts an exciting accompaniment to pan-fried cod. Serves 4.

INGREDIENTS

1 cup fresh basil leaves
2 tbsp toasted pine nuts
4 garlic cloves, peeled and chopped
1 tbsp lemon juice
$^1/_2$ cup olive oil
2 tbsp freshly shredded Parmesan cheese

METHOD

1 Place the basil leaves with the pine nuts,
   garlic, and lemon juice in a blender, and blend
   for 30 seconds.
2 Keeping the motor running, slowly add the
   olive oil and then stir in the Parmesan.
3 Spoon a little of the pesto over cooked pasta
   or white fish, such as charred cod (above).
   Garnish with basil leaves and serve the rest of
   the sauce separately.
4 If not using immediately, store in a sealed jar
   in the refrigerator for up to 10 days.

MARJORAM
Origanum majorana

OREGANO
Origanum vulgare

A widely used culinary herb, marjoram has found its way to our kitchens only in the past few decades. There are many different varieties, but sweet or knotted marjoram with its small, soft, sweet-spicy flavored, pale green leaves is the most widely used kinds in cooking.

A true herb of the Mediterranean, where it grows wild over the hills, marjoram is the herb of choice for cooking with traditional foods and recipes of the region, such as slow-baked lamb, plum tomatoes, eggplant, and bell peppers. It has small white or pink knots of flowers which are also edible.

Medicinally speaking, marjoram has a calming effect on the nerves, and is helpful in relieving tension and aiding digestion.

The ancient Egyptians prized oregano's power to heal, disinfect, and preserve, and today it is used to help fight colds and to relieve the symptoms of bronchitis as it contains the naturally occurring antiseptic, thymol. It is also helpful in relieving tension and aiding digestion. Oregano is also popular as a culinary herb and can be used in a variety of dishes. Related to marjoram, it has a stronger more robust flavor and requires sunny growing conditions with a well drained soil.

Oregano is a tallish, straggly plant with soft-textured, dark green, sweet-scented, peppery flavored leaves, it is widely used in the Mediterranean kitchen and has pretty white or pink flowers, which are also edible.

❦ CULINARY USES ❦

Sweet marjoram has a sweet, spicy flavor, and is an essential part of a bouquet garni (see page 152). The leaves can be chopped and added to soups, casseroles, egg or cheese dishes, fish, poultry, and vegetables. Potatoes, carrots, cabbage, tomatoes, bell peppers, and celery all benefit from a little marjoram. The flowers add a peppery flavor to salads or when sprinkled over soups just before serving. The leaves and flowers dry well, and chopped leaves can be frozen in the same way as chives (see page 22).

Caution: Avoid during pregnancy.

❦ CULINARY USES ❦

Oregano can easily overpower a dish if used excessively, so it is best kept for stronger flavored ingredients. It is particularly good in a garlicky tomato sauce and in rich meat and game dishes, and also blends well with chili and mushrooms. Use chopped leaves in salads and pasta dishes. Lay sprigs of oregano over meat on a barbecue or when roasting in the oven for a rich spicy and woody flavor. Both the leaves and flowers dry well, and chopped leaves can be frozen in the same way as chives (see page 22).

Caution: Avoid during pregnancy.

MELANZANE ALLA PARMIGIANA
(ITALIAN-BAKED EGGPLANT)

A delicious garlic-tomato-cheese-eggplant dish that is easy
to make and incredibly tasty. Serves 4.

INGREDIENTS

3 medium eggplants, about 2lb in total
Salt
²/₃ cup good quality olive oil
1 large onion, peeled and fine chopped
2 garlic cloves, peeled and fine chopped
2¹/₂ cups puréed tomatoes
2 tbsp fine chopped fresh oregano
Toasted pine nuts and Parmesan cheese shavings

METHOD

1 Preheat the oven to 350°F. Trim the eggplants
   and cut into slices about ³/₄ in. thick. Layer in
   a strainer, sprinkling with salt as you go. Set
   aside for 30 minutes.

2 Heat 1 tbsp oil and gently fry the onion and
   garlic for about 15 minutes until softened but
   not browned. Remove from the heat and
   stir in the puréed tomatoes and oregano.

3 Rinse the eggplant slices well and pat dry
   using paper towels. In a large skillet heat 2 to
   3 tbsp oil, and fry a few slices for 2 minutes
   on each side until lightly golden. Drain well
   on paper towels. Repeat, using more oil, as
   needed, to fry the remaining eggplant slices.

4 Spoon one-third of the sauce into the base
   of a large, shallow gratin dish. Lay half the
   eggplant slices on top and spoon over half
   the remaining sauce. Top with the remaining
   slices and spread over the rest of the sauce.

5 Stand on a cookie sheet. Bake in the oven for
   about 50 minutes until tender and golden.
   Sprinkle with toasted pine nuts and shavings
   of fresh Parmesan cheese if desired.

PARSLEY
Petroselinum crispum

*Grow as much parsley as you can. The more you pick the stalks from the base,
the more new shoots will appear. Incredibly versatile, the leaves can
be used in salads, soups, barbecued meats—you name it!*

Parsley was first mentioned in an early Greek herbal record in the third century BC as a medicinal herb to feed war horses. The Romans used it in cooking, and also as a deodorizer and a breath freshener. By the medieval period it was well known in Britain, and was taken to North America by the early settlers.

Parsley is rich in vitamins A (carotene) and C, also providing iron, calcium, magnesium, and chlorophyll (an antiseptic). Two common varieties used in the kitchen are curly parsley (*P. crispum*) with finely cut, crinkled, bunched leaves and a fresh taste, and French or continental parsley (*P. c. var. neapolitanum*) with flat, dark green leaves, coarser in texture and stronger in flavor.

Description and parts used

Parsley grows in a bushy clump about 15 in. high. It likes sun or partial shade. The leaves and soft stems are used in the kitchen.

❦ CULINARY USES ❦

Fresh parsley is one of the most versatile herbs with its own highly distinctive flavor. The stalks have a stronger flavor than the leaves, and are best used in casseroles, broths, and marinades.

A whole sprig is essential in a bouquet garni (see page 152). For soups, fish, meat, and poultry, use the freshly chopped leaves; they enhance the flavors of other ingredients, and are best added toward the end of the cooking time. Use as an ingredient in sauces for fish, cheese, and egg dishes, and add to French dressings.

As a garnish, parsley adds color and texture to any dish; sprinkle over chopped or use as a decorative sprig. It freezes well when fine chopped (see Chives, page 22).

TABBOULEH
(LEBANESE CRACKED WHEAT SALAD)

This tasty, nutritious, peppery, parsley–flavored recipe
is a refreshing appetizer on a warm summer day. Serves 4.

INGREDIENTS

1¹/₂ cups bulghur wheat
4 ripe tomatoes, about 8oz total weight, halved,
  seeds removed, and flesh fine chopped
4 scallions, trimmed and fine chopped
4 tbsp fine chopped fresh parsley
Salt and freshly ground black pepper
3 tbsp olive oil
3 tbsp lemon juice

METHOD

1 Place the bulghur wheat in a heatproof bowl.
   Cover with boiling water and set aside for
   30 minutes until tender and swollen. Drain if
   necessary and allow to cool.
2 Mix in the tomato, scallions, and parsley.
   Season well. Cover and chill until required.
3 To serve, pile on to serving plates and dress
   lightly with olive oil and lemon juice. Serve
   with warm pita bread and crisp lettuce.

SALAD BURNET
Sanguisorba minor (Poterium sanguisorba)

*A popular plant both for its culinary and its medicinal uses, it also makes
a good evergreen, particularly when grown as an
edging plant or in the wild garden.*

A native to Britain and Europe, the Pilgrim Fathers took it to New England where it was grown in gardens and then spread to the wild. Nowadays it is little used although in the seventeenth century Nicholas Culpeper claimed it was "so well known that it needeth no description." The plant is dainty, decorative, and surprisingly hardy. It has green flowering globes at the top of each stem, which turn bright pinkish-red in summer. The young leaves have a refreshingly sharp taste of nutty cucumber. As an infusion it can settle the stomach and aid digestion. Used on the skin it can soothe sunburn and inflamed skin conditions.

Description and parts used

Salad burnet will grow in the sun or light shade to 8–30 in. tall. The stems are long, grooved, and branching. The leaves line the stems and are lacy and fine-toothed, and are used in the kitchen.

❦ CULINARY USES ❦

Choose the inner softer leaves for the best flavor and texture—the outer ones soon become tough and bitter. Roughly chop the leaves and sprinkle over salads or freshly cooked vegetables for a refreshing note. Add to herb butters and soft cheese, or use in sprigs as a pretty garnish. Add at the beginning when cooking chicken or fish casseroles, or creamy soups. Also use in a creamy white sauce to go with white fish, and combine with tarragon and mint for added zing. Use instead of sage in a stuffing for chicken and pork. Sprigs can even be added to punches, iced fruit drinks, and dry wine cups for a cooling, refreshing effect.

The leaves dry well, but are best used fresh for cooking. Infuse in vinegar for a refreshing salad dressing.

ROSE
Rosa

Roses might be bare sticks and stems for most of the year, but the moment they come into flower everything perks up, and the flowers and hips are incredibly versatile.

Originating in Iran and important since the earliest times, the rose is widely used for its divine fragrance and beauty. Three varieties stand out for culinary use: the apothecary's rose or red rose of Lancaster (*Rosa gallica var. officinalis*), wild or dog rose (*R. canina*), and Japanese or Ramanas rose (*R. rugosa*).

Rose essence helps ease tension, while the hips contain a high level of vitamin C, and can be used to make a syrup for colds and coughs, and as a general tonic.

Description and parts used

Rosa gallica var. officinalis has lots of rose-pink, highly scented petals used to make oil and rosewater. *R. canina* has pink or white smaller petals that grow in a single layer; once the petals fall they leave behind the bright red hips, which are used in the kitchen. *R. rugosa* has deep pink aromatic petals used in medicine, and the hips can be used in the kitchen.

❧ CULINARY USES ❧

Use the scented petals with the bitter white heel removed. Sprinkle in salads or over desserts as an attractive, fragrant garnish. They are traditionally used either on their own or mixed with berry fruits to make perfumed preserves. The petals are steeped in liquid to make the essence that flavors the famous candy, Turkish Delight. They are also used to make syrups, vinegar, sorbets or flower sugar (see page 78), or candied petals for decorating cakes (see page 77).

To use the hips, remove the irritant hairs, then use to make tea, syrup, or wine. To make a purée of the hips, sweeten, add lemon juice, and serve with roasted lamb. The petals can be dried, candied, or pickled in vinegar. The hips can also be dried and used to make tea.

ROSEMARY
Rosmarinus officinalis

*Given a sunny site and good drainage, you can grow an impressive,
evergreen rosemary shrub with plenty of presence, and you will have
an endless supply of herbs for the kitchen.*

Rosemary grows wild on Mediterranean coasts, its name being the Latin for "dew of the sea," a reference to its blue flowers. It has been used by cooks and herbalists for centuries, and has acquired a reputation for strengthening the memory. It is often used as a symbol of remembrance. There are many varieties of rosemary, and all have a resinous aroma in their stems and leaves.

Rosemary contains strong antiseptic and anti-inflammatory oils, and acts as a circulatory stimulant with balancing and calming effects on the digestive system.

Description and parts used

A hardy, evergreen shrub growing from 3–8 ft. tall, depending on variety. It likes sun and shelter. The woody stems are packed with needlelike, dark green, leathery leaves. The edible flowers can be white, lilac, blue, or pink (see page 78).

❦ CULINARY USES ❦

Rosemary can overpower a dish because it is a very strong, aromatic herb. Use whole sprigs under roasted lamb or placed inside a chicken or whole fish. Finely chop the leaves and add to tomato-based soups, to boiled ham and any meat or game casserole. Chop finely and add to cookie and biscuit mixes or bread dough (see recipe opposite). Add sprigs to flavor a sugar syrup for pouring over poached peaches, or add to preserves for serving with game.

The leaves dry well on the stalks and can then be stripped off to store, being crumbled at the last minute to release the aroma. Because it can be picked all year, there is no need for freezing. Infuse in oil or vinegar with other herbs and spices to give a resinous flavor.

ROSEMARY FOCACCIA

An Italian bread topped with herbs, similar in consistency to pizza dough. Outside Italy it's used for sandwiches. Makes one $1/3$-in. x 9-in. round loaf.

INGREDIENTS

4$1/4$ cups very strong white bread flour
1$1/2$ tsp salt
1$1/2$ tsp superfine sugar
1 tbsp fine chopped fresh rosemary
2$1/2$ tsp active dry yeast
Scant 1 cup water, slightly warm
Scant $1/2$ cup good quality olive oil
A few sprigs fresh rosemary
1–2 tsp coarse sea salt to taste

METHOD

1 Sift the flour, 1$1/2$ tsp salt, and sugar into a bowl and stir in the chopped rosemary and yeast. Make a well in the center and pour in the water and 6 tablespoons of the oil. Mix to make a soft dough.

2 Turn onto a lightly floured surface and knead for 5 minutes until smooth. Place in a floured bowl, cover loosely, and leave in a warm place for about an hour until it has doubled in size.

3 Re-knead the dough and press into a greased, deep-sided, 9 in. round pan, cover loosely and leave in a warm place for about 40 minutes until it has doubled in size. Preheat the oven to 400°F.

4 Grease the end of a wooden spoon, and press into the dough to indent the surface. Brush with oil, press small sprigs of rosemary into the top, and sprinkle with coarse salt to taste.

5 Bake for about 30 minutes until the focaccia is well raised and golden, and sounds hollow when tapped. Transfer to a wire rack and drizzle with remaining oil. Best served warm.

SORREL
Rumex acetosa

A multipurpose perennial, sorrel can be used in a wide range of recipes including soups, salads, and sauces, and can even be wrapped around steaks or added to marinades.

There are two main varieties, broad-leaf or garden sorrel (*R. acetosa*), and buckler leaf or French sorrel (*R. scutatus*). Unfortunately, both types are often called French or garden sorrel, so always check the leaves' flavor and shape before buying. The leaves of both are used in the kitchen.

R. acetosa is more familiar, and grows wild all over Europe, Scandinavia, Asia, and North America. Young leaves have little flavor; acidity develops as they age. *R. scutatus* (preferred by French cooks) is native to southern Europe, Germany, and Switzerland. The leaves are finer and less pointed, and the flavor is less acidic.

Description and parts uses

R. acetosa has large, spear-shaped leaves, and the flavor is astringent and lemony. It grows to 2–4 ft. in sun or light shade. *R. scutatus* is smaller at 6–18 in., and likes full sun and shelter.

🌿 CULINARY USES 🌿

One of the original uses for sorrel was as a salad herb, so try adding a few young leaves to other green salad leaves and herbs to give a distinctive edge. In cooked dishes, the leaves wilt quickly, like spinach and watercress, and are therefore best added as close to serving as possible. Add a few leaves to soups, sauces, cooked pasta dishes, and cooked potatoes.

Sorrel also goes well with eggs—simply sauté in butter and stir into scrambled eggs, omelets, or soufflés. When cooking, change the water once to reduce the acidity.

Traditionally, sorrel is also used to make a green sauce to go with oily fish (see opposite) and rich meats. Sorrel is best used fresh (the dried kind has little flavor).

SORREL SAUCE

This rich, creamy, lemony sauce is ideal with all kinds of mild or strong fish, such as grilled trout, adding instant zest. Serves 6.

INGREDIENTS

¹/₂ lb sorrel, stalks trimmed
4 tbsp butter
4 tbsp all-purpose flour
1¹/₄ cups fish or vegetable broth
Zest and juice 1 small lemon, finely minced
1 cup heavy cream
2 medium egg yolks
1 tsp superfine sugar
Salt and freshly ground black pepper

METHOD

1 Rinse the sorrel leaves and pack into a saucepan while still wet. Heat, stirring occasionally, until steam rises, then cover and cook gently for 2 to 3 minutes until the leaves are wilted.

2 Rinse well, then press against the side of a colander to remove as much water as possible. Chop fine and set aside.

3 Melt the butter and stir in the flour. Cook for 1 minute. Remove from the heat and gradually stir in the broth. Return to the heat and cook, stirring, until the sauce has thickened. Cool for 10 minutes then transfer to a blender. Add the remaining ingredients, including the chopped sorrel, and blend for a few seconds until smooth.

4 Return to a clean saucepan, heat through gently, until hot but not boiling. Serve with grilled trout (as above), salmon, or tuna.

SAGE
Salvia officinalis

Sage is one of the main ingredients for a cook's garden. Though it comes from the Mediterranean, it's easily grown given a sheltered hotspot and excellent drainage.

Sage was a cherished herb in China, Persia, and throughout the Roman Empire, being regarded as sacred and associated with long life. The botanical name comes from the Latin *salvare*, which means "to save or cure."

Sage has a robust flavor and is used to aid digestion. It also has anti-inflammatory and antiseptic qualities.

Description and parts used

There are many varieties of sage, and all make attractive garden plants for their delightfully fragrant foliage and flowers. All are woody-stemmed with soft, downy leaves and spikes of flowers loved by bees. Sage varies in height, depending on variety, from 2–3 ft. Common sage (*S. officianalis*) is the most widely used in the kitchen, and is highly aromatic and pungent. It has pale gray-green leaves and violet-pink flowers. The leaves and soft stems are used in the kitchen.

☙ CULINARY USES ☙

Traditionally sage is used to flavor cheese, sausages, stuffings, and the Italian dish saltimbocca. Use sparingly because the flavor quickly dominates. Combine with other strong flavors, such as liver, rich meats, duck, and sausages for best results. Sage butter is delicious melted over broiled pork or duck. The leaves can be finely chopped and used traditionally as a seasoning for a stuffing. Deep-fried sage leaves can be used as a garnish for soups, casseroles, and pasta dishes. Small bunches of fresh young leaves can be dipped in batter, deep fried, then served with cream, sugar, and fresh orange. They are best used fresh or dried rather than frozen.

Caution: Avoid during pregnancy because large quantities can be toxic.

PORK WITH SAGE AND CHARRED-APPLE RELISH

The tartness of dried cranberries works surprisingly well with the
traditional combination of sage and pork. Serves 4.

INGREDIENTS

Four 4-oz slices pork loin, pounded thin
2 tsp wholegrain mustard
$^1/_2$ cup clear apple juice
A few fresh sage leaves, lightly crushed
8 oz apples, peeled, cored, and chopped fine
2 tbsp dried cranberries or raisins
1 tbsp cider vinegar
1 tsp wholegrain mustard
$^2/_3$ cup sour cream

METHOD

1 Trim the pork if necessary, wipe, and place
in a shallow dish. Blend the mustard with
the apple juice and pour over the pork slices.
Scatter the pork mixture with the sage leaves,
cover lightly, and leave in the refrigerator
for about 30 minutes.

2 Lightly brush or spray a griddle pan with
oil then place on a moderate heat until hot.
Add the apple pieces and cook for 2 to 3
minutes or until soft and slightly charred,
but not pulpy.

3 Remove from the pan and add to the
remaining relish ingredients, stir well, and
set aside.

4 Drain the escalopes and cook in the hot pan
for 3 to 5 minutes each side or until the pork
is done.

5 Slice the pork and place on a bed of spinach
leaves. Serve with the apple relish, potatoes,
and freshly cooked vegetables. Garnish with
sage leaves.

ELDER
Sambucus nigra

A tall, upright, bushy shrub, elder can easily be grown at the edge of a garden or as part of a wild hedge, and produces lovely flat heads of white flowers and jewel-like clusters of dark fruit.

An important and valuable shrub, elder was once called "the medicine chest of the people" because it was believed to cure most common complaints. Elder is a bitter, pungent, cooling herb that lowers a high temperature, reduces inflammation, soothes irritation, and has diuretic properties. The scented flowers and dark purple berries have anti-catarrhal agents, while the leaves are insecticidal and antiseptic. Elderflower water can be used to fade freckles and as an effective skin toner. The flowers are also used in skin lotions.

Description and parts used

A deciduous shrub with oval serrated leaves, it grows to about 15 ft. tall. If left unpicked, by early fall, the fruit forms drooping bunches of purple-black, juicy berries. Historically, all parts of the shrub are used, but modern usage favors the flowers. Pick the flowers in bunches, and use as soon as possible.

🌿 CULINARY USES 🌿

The flowerheads add a muscatel grape-scented flavor to fruit jellies, preserves, and compotes, and go particularly well with gooseberries. Dip whole heads in a light batter and deep fry. Serve sprinkled with sugar as a crisp, flowery fritter.

Elderflower cordial (see recipe opposite) is a popular soft drink, and makes a lovely cooling spritzer or "champagne" when mixed with chilled, dry, sparkling white wine. Preserves, cordials, wine, and sauces can be made from elder fruits, but always cook the fruit first before eating.

All parts of the elder are best used fresh, although the berries freeze well and can be dried, making them less bitter. **Caution: Avoid the seeds which can be toxic.**

ELDERFLOWER CORDIAL

A refreshing, fruity drink made from fresh garden ingredients, which keeps well. Makes about 2 cups undiluted cordial.

INGREDIENTS
¼ lb elder flowerheads, trimmed and washed
2 cups water
¾ lb superfine sugar

METHOD
1 Put the flowerheads in a saucepan and pour over the water. Bring to a boil, cover, and simmer gently for 30 minutes.

2 Strain through cheesecloth and return to a clean saucepan.

3 Add the sugar and heat gently, stirring, until dissolved. Bring to a boil and simmer, uncovered, for 15 minutes until syrupy and lightly golden.

4 Pour into a hot, sterilized bottled, seal and cool. Label and store in the refrigerator for up to 3 months. Serve diluted with water.

SASSAFRAS
Sassafras albidum

No ordinary hardy, edge-of-woodland American tree, sassafras has an abundance of talents and can be used for just about everything from making root beer to making perfume.

A common deciduous tree, sassafras is found in many states from Maine to Florida. The leaves are so strongly scented that they apparently guided Christopher Columbus to the shores of the New World. Before the arrival of European settlers, American Indians chewed the root for its restorative properties.

Sassafras was probably one of the first medicinal herbs to reach Europe around 1560, and was discovered to have antirheumatic, antiseptic and diuretic properties.

Today, the volatile oil extracted from the bark of the root is used commercially as a perfume and flavoring.

Description and parts used

The sassafras tree can grow to a height of around 70 ft. It has gnarly bark and leaves of various shapes, up to 6 in. long. The leaves, bark, and roots are used in the kitchen and food industry.

❦ CULINARY USES ❦

The leaves contain a gummy mucilage and they can be dried and powdered to make filé powder. This powder is used to thicken and flavor soups, casseroles, and gumbos in the Louisiana region of North America. Filé gumbo, a thick okra soup, is probably the best-known dish from this region. The powdered leaves give a flavor similar to fennel or celery.

Also in the Southern states, shavings of sassafras wood and roots are used to make deep red sassafras tea, and a jelly made from the tea is used to serve with meat. Sassafras root is used commercially as one of the flavorings in root beer. Unless you have a sassafras tree in your garden, you'll only be able to obtain the dry herb.

SAVORY
Satureja

There are several species, but the two best-known are summer savory
(S. hortensis), which has a highly aromatic, peppery flavor, and
winter savory (S. montana) with its sharper, spicier edge.

One of the oldest flavoring herbs, the Greeks called savory "thymbra," and the Romans used it as a medicine and to flavor sauces and vinegars. They spread the herb around Europe, and savory has since been used in the kitchens of northern European, particularly as a flavoring for stuffings.

Summer savory was one of the first plants introduced to North America by early colonists, and is now grown commercially in California. Savory also has antiseptic properties and is said to benefit the whole digestive tract.

Description and parts used

Savory is a hardy, evergreen subshrub that grows to a height of about 15 in. The winter variety has woody, hairy, branching stems with numerous aromatic, narrow-pointed, dark green leaves. Summer savory is a sparser plant with longer, narrow, dark green leaves.

❦ CULINARY USES ❦

Summer savory is a good flavoring for poultry, meat, soups, eggs, salads, and sauces—simply chop finely and add at the beginning of cooking. It also makes an attractive garnish instead of parsley. Summer savory is known as the "bean herb" in parts of Europe because it enhances the flavors of pulses, beans, and lentils. The leaves of winter savory are stronger in flavor, so use sparingly with sausages or add to marinades and stuffings. It can also be used to flavor relishes, giving a spicy edge with rich meat.

Winter savory makes a good salt substitute if you're on a low-sodium diet. The oil has a sharp, bitter flavor, and is used commercially to flavor salami. Savory leaves dry well, and fresh sprigs can be preserved in oil or vinegar to give a peppery note.

GARDEN THYME
Thymus vulgaris

There is a huge range of thymes, from the low-growing spreaders to shrubbier kinds, garden thyme being one of the best. They make large mounds of leafy growth, most with terrific scent.

Thyme is highly aromatic and a natural preservative. The ancient Egyptians used thyme as part of their embalming rituals; Roman soldiers bathed in thyme-scented waters to promote vigor; and the herb was used in the Roman kitchen, its use spreading around Europe.

The best varieties include wild creeping thyme (*T. praecox subsp. arcticis*) with its mild, subtle thyme scent; broad-leaf thyme (*T. pulegioides*) with its stronger, more robust flavor; garden thyme (*T. vulgaris*), which is the most aromatic; and Azores thyme (*T. caespititius*) with its lovely citrus-pine scent. Lemon thyme (*T. x citriodorus*) and caraway thyme (*T. herba-barona*) speak for themselves.

Description and parts used

A small, evergreen shrub 3–15 in. in height. The stems are woody with branches of many fine-pointed, green leaves. The leaves are often used while still on the stems.

❧ CULINARY USES ❧

Thyme has a distinctive, strong flavor. A sprig of thyme is a "must" in a bouquet garni and for flavoring soups, broths, and marinades. Good for sprinkling over roasting root vegetables and field mushrooms (see recipe opposite). Add chopped leaves to meat, fish, and shellfish dishes, or to marinades. Place a few sprigs under any roasting meat or on top of barbecued steaks to imbue a woody, fresh aroma.

Thyme dries well on the stalks, but you can also strip leaves off to store, then crumble into cooking just before serving to release the aroma. Infuse in oil or vinegar with garlic to give a fragrant, woody note. As it can be picked all-year, there is no need to freeze garden thyme. **Caution: Avoid thyme oil and infusions during pregnancy.**

GARLIC MUSHROOMS WITH THYME

These juicy mouthfuls of garlic- and thyme-flavored mushrooms will warm you up on winter evenings. Serves 4.

INGREDIENTS

1¹/₂ tbsp olive oil

2 cloves garlic, peeled and minced

2³/₄ cups (7oz) button mushrooms

2 tbsp white wine

1 tsp tomato paste

¹/₂ tsp fresh thyme leaves plus extra for garnishing

Salt and freshly ground black pepper

METHOD

1 Pour the olive oil into a skillet. Gently fry the garlic in the oil for about 1 minute, then add the mushrooms and toss to coat in the oil.

2 Stir the wine and tomato paste together and pour over the mushrooms, then add the thyme and season with salt and pepper. Cook gently for 15 to 20 minutes, stirring occasionally, until most of the juices have evaporated and the mushrooms are juicy and glossy but not wet.

3 Transfer to a serving dish and sprinkle with fresh thyme leaves before serving.

FENUGREEK
Trigonella foenum-graecum

A must for anyone interested in Middle-Eastern cooking, fenugreek leaves and toasted seeds are used as an essential flavoring, while others rate the plant highly for its wide-ranging medicinal uses.

A leguminous plant related to clover, fenugreek is native to southern Europe and Asia and is widely grown as a condiment crop. Archaeological evidence suggests that the ancient Egyptians were using the herb for eating, healing, and embalming. The Greeks and Romans also cooked with the herb and used it in medicine. The leaves have a slightly bitter but pleasant taste when young, and when dry take on a sweet, haylike aroma. In fact, the botanical name for the species means "Greek hay." The leguminous part of the plant is the seed pods from which fenugreek seeds are dried and used as a spice (see page 145).

Description and parts used

A tall, thin, light green stem with short leaf branches, fenugreek grows to about 12 ft. The leaves resemble the three-leaf clover. The seed pods are long, thin, and pointed, and may contain up to 20 seeds.

❦ CULINARY USES ❦

You can sprout your own seeds, just like mustard and cress, to grow fresh, young leaf sprouts that add a real zing when tossed into salads or added to sandwich fillers. Young leaves are a popular vegetable in India and are the flavoring in the flaky bread, paratha. Older, larger leaf sprays can be boiled or steamed like spinach, and used in a vegetable curry. The leaves are a staple vegetable in Yemen and are used along with the spice to flavor sauces.

The dried leaves are known as methi, which has a strong, bitter flavor. Methi is used in Indian and Middle Eastern cooking to flavor starchy vegetables, rice dishes, fish, and tandoori dishes. The leaves dry well but they should be well sealed before storing because they emit a strong aroma.

NASTURTIUM (INDIAN CRESS)
Tropaeolum majus

*Typically seen romping up a trellis, through a shrub or hedge, or even across
a path, it makes a flamboyant addition to the flower garden,
although it's increasingly being recognized as an herb.*

Nasturtium originated in Peru, and was taken to Europe by the Spanish in the sixteenth century. From there it gradually made its way with European settlers to North America. It was known as "Indian cress" because the peppery, pungent flavor of the older leaves reminded settlers of cress or watercress.

The English word nasturtium derives from the Latin for "twisted nose," which perhaps hints at the facial expression adopted when eating it! The whole plant is used in the kitchen but, medicinally, the leaves contain vitamin C, and can double up as an antiseptic.

Description and parts used

A trailing, spreading, vigorous annual that grows to 3–10 ft. in height and width. The mid-green leaves are round and flat with yellow-green veins, and are beautifully set off by the very attractive yellow, red, or orange, trumpetlike, late summer flowers.

❦ CULINARY USES ❦

Young nasturium leaves taste a bit like watercress, but older leaves have a more pronounced peppery flavor. Toss small leaves whole into salads or add to sandwiches with sliced ham and chicken for extra bite. They can be used as an alternative to arugula but they are best mixed with a milder leaf, such as lamb's lettuce. Chop large leaves and mix with egg mayonnaise or with soft cheese to make a tasty sandwich filling.

Finely chopped leaves make a good flavoring for French dressing, to pep up salads or to pour over chicken, fish, and seafood. The unripe seeds can be pickled in vinegars, and are a good substitute for capers. The leaves are best used fresh rather than frozen or dried.

FLOWERING HERBS FOR CULINARY USE

Flowers give special appeal to any dish to which they are added, but remember to consider their color and flavor when mixing them with other ingredients so they harmonize.

Many herb flowers are edible, and some of the tastiest are listed here. Often quite small, these little morsels will make any dish more attractive and give added herbal flavor, often with a peppery edge.

Chive (*Allium schoenoprasum*)

A pretty pink, spiky flower with a mild onion flavor. Use to garnish soups and entrées, and toss into salads and cooked pasta for a colorful and tasty addition.

Mustard (*Brassica*)

Used since prehistoric times, mustard is probably most well known for its seed, which is used as a spice (see pages 94–95) that is particularly good with ham and sausages. The flowers offer a mild mustard flavor without the heat. They are bright yellow, and grow in four-petal clusters at the tops of long, willowy stems. Add to sandwiches or toss into salads for a little spicy "bite."

Wild carnation (*Dianthus caryophyllus*)

Also known as clove pink, the wild carnation was regarded as a flower of divinity to the Greeks, while the Romans made coronets and garlands with it. The flowers have long been used as a pretty garnish or can be floated in drinks. The single or double flowers can be white, pink, or purple depending on variety. It has a sweet, clovelike perfume. Remove the bitter white heel before using to flavor salads, fruit pies and sandwiches. Use to flavor sugar, preserves, oil, vinegar, and wine. The flower petals can be candied (see opposite).

Sweet arugula (*Hesperis matronalis*)

A native of Italy, the herb is grown as a pretty cottage garden flower with a sweet scent, although it can be found growing wild all over Europe and North America. The abundant blooms appear in midsummer and consist of four petals in purple, mauve, pink, or white. Add to salads for a touch of sweetness, or use the flowerheads whole as a decoration for desserts and fruit salads. You can dry the flowers for winter use.

Hyssop (*Hyssopus officinalis*)

The flowers grow in clusters up one side of the plant stem. They are usually rich blue but can also be pink, purple and, occasionally, white. The tiny blooms inject an aromatic addition to a leaf salad or can be used to make a flower sugar (see opposite) for sprinkling over a cranberry compote.

Myrtle (*Myrtus communis*)

Sweetly scented myrtle flowers have white petals with golden stamens. Pick carefully to remove the bitter green back, and add to fruit salads. Dried buds can be powdered and used as a sweet seasoning for fruit.

Sweet basil (*Ocimum basilicum*)

The best variety for flowers is the purple *O. b. var. purpurascens* with its flavored, pale pink petals. Toss into salads, pasta dishes, or add to oils and vinegars for dressings.

Scented geranium (*Pelargonium*)

Most pelargoniums (not be confused with hardy geraniums) originate from the Cape of Good Hope in Africa. They spread to Britain in the seventeenth century and to North America in the eighteenth century. By the mid-nineteenth century, they had become widely used in the perfume industry.

There are many varieties and many are highly prized. The aromas range from the rose-, apple-, and lemon-scented to peppermint and nutmeg.

CANDIED FLOWERS AND LEAVES

A novel and beautiful way to use leaves, making an eye-catching addition to a tray of tasty snacks.

METHOD

1 Pick your chosen flowers or leaves on a sunny, dry day. Remove the stalks and the white bases from the flowerheads.
2 Lightly beat an egg white until it starts to foam. Dip each flower or leaf in the egg white. If you have the time and patience, for a finer effect, you can apply the egg white using a small brush. Then cover in superfine sugar.
3 Place on a sheet of waxed paper on a wire cooling rack. Cover with another sheet of waxed paper and place in a very low oven, with the door ajar, for a few hours until the flowers and leaves are dry and crisp. Store in an airtight container until needed to decorate cakes and desserts.

❦ CULINARY USES ❦

Always use flowers from flowering herbs raw because heat quickly makes them wilt.

Try tossing the flowers into salads, floating them on soups and drinks, or scatter a few onto cooked food just before serving.

Citrus-scented varieties of flowering herbs, such as *Pelargonium crispum*, can be used to make tea and flavor sorbets.

Blossoms can be pickled lightly in vinegar to preserve them and to make floral-scented salad dressings.

Flowers also dry well for later use in potpourri, but are best picked from the plant just before flowering.

Some flowering herbs can stand being candied for decoration (see page 77).

The essential oil is used in aromatherapy. In the kitchen, the leaves and flowers add fragrance and flavor to a variety of dishes.

Pelargoniums grow to 1–3 ft., and need full sun and good drainage. They grow well in pots and can survive cold, wet winters if moved indoors. The leaves are chiefly used in the kitchen, but don't ignore the flowers.

Cowslip and primrose
(*Primula veris* and *Primula vulgaris*)

Heralding spring and early summer, the sight of these two blooms never fails to lift the spirits. The cowslip has golden petals that grow in bunches at the top of long stems, while the primrose has an individual, heartshaped, pale yellow flower on each stem. The sweet flavor of cowslip has been used for centuries to make wine and preserves, while the primrose can be eaten raw in salads, or candied (see page 77). It is often used to decorate sweet pastries.

Rosemary (*Rosmanirus officinalis*)
Depending on the variety, rosemary flowers can be white, pale pink, lilac, or blue. They are small and aromatic. Pick out the little flowerheads and toss into salads and pasta dishes. Candy them and use for decoration, or pound with sugar and mix into fruit purée with heavy cream to make a fruit fool.

Sage (*Salvia officinalis*)
The deep-throated flowerheads are generally mauve-blue, but they can also be white or pink. Apart from adding a sage flavor to a salad, they are delicious scattered over soft cheeses as a garnish, and can be lightly infused in hot water to make a light balsamic tea.

Thyme (*Thymus*)
Pink to pale lilac clusters of tiny blooms make a pretty addition to a salad, adding a sweet, aromatic, woody flavor.

Nasturtium (*Tropaeolum majus*)
The stunning red, orange, or yellow flowerheads make a spectacular garnish on the plate, or can be added to salads for their mild, peppery, cresslike flavor. The flower buds can be pickled and eaten in the same way as capers.

Sweet violet (*Viola odorata*)
The Greeks chose sweet violet as their symbol of fertility, while the Romans enjoyed sweet violet wine. It is a delicate and beautiful spring flower with a prominent, heady, sweet scent that has been used in cosmetics, drinks, desserts, and syrups for centuries. The violet or white blooms appear from late winter to midspring and are commonly candied (see page 77).

Garden pansy (*V. x wittrockiana*)
A cultivated variety of violet, the garden pansy has much larger blooms and grows in an array of bright colors. It makes a bold statement as a decoration or salad ingredient, although the flavor is less perfumed and slightly sweet.

FLOWER SUGAR

Quick and simple, this inventive, imaginative idea perks up a wide range of snacks. Serves 4–6.

INGREDIENTS
$^1/_2$ cup superfine sugar
2 tbsp hyssop, myrtle, or scented pelargonium flowers

METHOD
1 Place the sugar and herb flowers in a mortar and grind with a pestle, or place in a bowl and blend with the end of a wooden rolling pin.
2 Place in an airtight container and store in a cool, dry place for up to a month.
3 Use to sprinkle over cookies, shortbread, cakes, or to flavor syrups and sorbets. Makes an attractive addition to a cup of herbal or fruit tea.

Spice
Directory

A BRIEF HISTORY OF SPICES

SPICES THROUGH THE AGES

There is something evocative about spices that goes way beyond their culinary or medicinal uses. Who can hear the words "Spice Islands" without feeling a shiver of excitement, a call of adventure and discovery? Wars were fought over spices, and empires lost in their cause. Explorers set out to find the strange and exotic lands where they came from, traveling all over Egypt, China, Arabia, Persia, India, Greece, and Zanzibar.

Some spices were worth more than precious metals and gems, with both frankincense and myrrh being considered so valuable that they were included in the three gifts the Wise Men brought to the baby Jesus.

Today, spices are essential ingredients in any good cook's kitchen, and commercially they are still valuable commodities in the manufacture of perfumes, incense, oils, cosmetics, preservatives, and flavorings.

World history without the history of spices would be very different. Spices have been directly responsible for wars, the opening of trade routes, papal edicts and decrees, medicinal cures, cosmetic preparations, and religious rituals, not to mention some of the world's most delicious cuisine. And they have been traded and used for longer than most people realize.

The beginnings of the spice trade

At least 5,000 years ago in China, Emperor Shen Nung wrote a medical treatise extoling the virtues of ginger, cassia, anise seed, and turmeric. He founded spice markets, and his longevity is attributed to the vast amounts of spices he used in his own food. Confucius was advising his disciples, around 550 BC, not to eat any food that had not been prepared properly with spices.

At about the same time, the Arab world was trading spices with India, and the Indian spice ports on the Malabar Coast were doing a roaring trade in cardamom, ginger (used on boats to ward off scurvy), turmeric, peppers, sesame, and cumin. Arabian traders also bought spices from other places—cinnamon from Sri Lanka; mace, nutmeg, and cloves from the East Indies; and myrrh from East Africa, though they also produced their own frankincense.

The trade routes were long and arduous, and involved traveling by camel caravan from Calcutta, and sea journeys through the Persian

Gulf. It was a profitable and lucrative trade. Naturally the traders kept the exact location of the spice lands to themselves, and even invented fantastic and ludicrous stories of where the spices came from to throw others off the trail. They bought and sold all over Egypt, Persia, Afghanistan, and the Mediterranean—and from there the spices were introduced to Europe.

The Greeks and Romans

In ancient Greece and Rome, spices were considered so valuable and important that they were used to flavor just about everything. The Greeks and Romans also wrote extensively about their cosmetic and medicinal applications. Nero is said to have burned a year's supply of cinnamon at his wife's funeral (not just his own supply but also that of the whole of Rome).

Traditionally, the Greeks liked their food plain and unadorned, and Greek philosophers maintained that although pleasure was what life was all about, it should be simple and enjoyed in moderation. However, by the time the Greek civilization fell into decline, the Greeks were spicing up their food like everyone else.

As the Roman Empire spread throughout Europe, the soldiers took their spices with them and introduced them to the indigenous populations. When the Empire collapsed and the Romans retreated to Rome, they left behind a rich legacy of spice use. With the Romans gone, 700 years of dullness fell on the European palate. The spice trade continued in Asia, but the art of spices was lost in Europe. It wasn't until the crusaders returned from Palestine in the twelfth century that Europe finally woke up again, and the spice trade flourished once more.

The Italian Renaissance

Medieval cooking took on a new emphasis and originality—everything had to be spicy and highly colored, despite the fact that the spices were so expensive. At one time a horse was valued at the same price as a pound of saffron, while a sheep could be bartered for a pound of ginger, and a cow for two pounds of mace. Pepper was so highly valued that its price was measured in individual peppercorns, and they were even used to pay taxes and rent. Later, when peppercorns became less valuable, tenants who were still allowed to pay their rent in peppercorns were considered extremely lucky, and the term "peppercorn rent" came to mean the exact opposite of what it did originally.

The spice explorers

At this time, the Arab world still controlled the flow and trade of spices. But at the beginning of the thirteenth century Marco Polo set out from Venice to find a new trade route to China—one that would bypass the Arab traders. When he returned 25 years later, he brought with him fabulous wealth and treasures from the court of Chinese Emperor Kubla Khan, and many spices. In fact, nobody back in Venice believed that he had actually made such a fantastic journey until he cooked a magnificent meal for his friends with the new, exotic spices that he had brought back with him.

However, it would be another two centuries before Europeans rebelled against the exorbitant price of many spices, and decided to do something about it.

Venice's trading agreements with the Arab world kept the prices artificially high and provided the Venetians with much of their wealth. This meant the Venetian traders had a vested interest in maintaining the status quo, so it fell to Prince Henry of Portugal, known as Henry the Navigator, to open up new trade routes. In the days of primitive sailing ships that had never left the sight of land, Prince Henry financed and equipped expeditions to sail around Africa and find a route to the Indian Ocean. Unfortunately he died without seeing a successful voyage but, by 1480, the Portuguese had learned how to sail before the wind—and were now able to sail to India. The first expeditions arrived there in 1497.

Meanwhile an unknown Italian, Christopher Columbus, claimed he could reach India ahead of the Portuguese—not by sailing around Africa, but by sailing westward into the unknown Atlantic. Employed by the Spanish, he set sail in 1492 and, three months later, landed in the West Indies, so-called because he initially thought he had reached India. He then reached the Americas and, although disappointed that he hadn't succeeded in his mission, he was soon rewarded by what he found there. He returned with allspice from the West Indies, chilies from Mexico, and vanilla from Central America. Almost simultaneously, two spice routes had opened up—and the trade wars started.

The Spanish and Portuguese found so many ways to interfere with each other's spice trade that the pope was obliged to issue an edict dividing the world into two spice halves: Spain could have everything to the west of an imaginary line in the Atlantic Ocean, while Portugal could have everything to the east.

The Spanish then employed Magellan (who was Portuguese) to sail westward with five ships and more than 200 sailors to find another route to the Moluccas and the island of Bandaas. They argued that if they approached from the west, they wouldn't upset the pope and would still be able to capture the lucrative clove and nutmeg market! Magellan did not make it back to Spain, but one of his ships did by rounding the coast of South America.

The British, Dutch, and Americans

These powers entered the market in a big way. The Dutch founded the Dutch East India Company to trade directly with India for spices, and the British financed Francis Drake to sail around the world to find another passage to China. War broke out between England and Spain over trade routes, which led to the defeat of the Spanish Armada in 1588 and the formation of the British East India Company.

In 1658 the Dutch fought and beat the Portuguese for the cinnamon trade of Ceylon, and added the pepper ports of Malabar and Java. By 1690 the Dutch had a monopoly on the clove trade, but only because they burned all the clove trees growing on other islands except for Aboyna. They defended this monopoly for 60 years until a Frenchman managed to smuggle a ripe fruit off the island and took it to the French colonies, where it was successfully planted.

By the end of the eighteenth century, the British had ousted the Dutch from India, and London briefly became the center of the world's spice trade. But that was not to last long. During the American War of Independence, the Americans had developed swift sailing warships, known as clippers, to defeat the might of the British navy. After the war, these ships sat idle for only a short while before they were again used against the British—this time to sail to the East Indies, and break Britain's spice monopoly before it really took hold.

SPICES FOR HEALTH

In the thirteenth century Pope Innocent III passed an edict that no ecclesiastic should practice medicine for profit, or shed blood in any way. This edict meant that surgery passed into the hands of lay people, mostly barbers, while priests and monks devoted their time to the search for cures based on natural plants. In effect, it meant that there was a division between surgeons and herbalists, the latter in holy orders concerning themselves with the theoretical aspects of medicine. This led to a surge in interest in the plants that had an effect on a patient's condition.

As the Spanish and Portuguese explorers came back from the New World, the plants and spices that they carried were seized on as being miraculous, and in certain cases, their medicinal qualities were exaggerated. However, many spices do have a natural warming effect and are used against colds, coughs, and flu symptoms.

In this book, you'll find information for each spice entry regarding specific remedies and properties, but always remember that any illnesses that you would not normally treat at home should not be treated with spice remedies. Consult a qualified medical physician if in doubt.

SPICES TODAY

After the ferocious spice trading that went on for 600 years, the situation today may seem a little tame. Spices seem to have gradually gone out of favor, and no longer do we seek new spice routes or wage wars over them. But maybe we have grown used to the less-than-fresh, commercially prepared spices that can be bought in any supermarket. Maybe, thanks to the introduction of the refrigerator into virtually every household in the Western world, we have so much fresh food that we no longer need spices to mask the taste of less palatable food. Spices, however, are not just a cover up. They provide a varied and scintillating range of tastes and experiences, and it may be time we started grinding fresh spices and reawakened our taste buds to their richness.

The current cultivation and distribution of spices is fascinating. Who would have thought that the chilies discovered in Mexico would have been taken to India and incorporated into curries? This has occurred to such an extent that most people today believe that Indian chilies are native to India when in fact they come from the Americas. What is more, who would have

thought that Canada would become the world's largest mustard producer?

Spices are no longer regarded as wonders of medicine, but they still play an important part in the manufacture of many cosmetics and perfumes, and are grown commercially for their coloring and preservative properties. Cloves still come from Madagascar and Zanzibar. Nutmeg and mace are no longer the main crops of the Moluccas, but instead are grown on a large scale on the Caribbean island of Grenada.

Cooking with spices

Spices have been used for as long as humans have been cooking food. As culinary techniques developed beyond one-pot cooking, more variety in the diet could be achieved, and this meant variety, experimentation, and a vast explosion in the use of spices.

Nowadays, spices are indispensable ingredients in all types of dishes, adding and enhancing existing flavors while at the same time aiding digestion. They complement almost any type of meal, from salads, casseroles, and soups to desserts, cakes, pickles, and drinks.

CHOOSING, STORING, AND PREPARATION

Spices are flown and shipped regularly all over the world. They are usually picked, processed, packed, and labeled in their country of origin, so that they are as fresh as possible when they reach their final destination. Here are a few hints and tips to remember when choosing, preparing and using spices to help you get the maximum amount of flavor from them.

Buy spices that are as fresh as possible—check that the packaging is intact, that the product is well within its sell-by date, and that the spices look bright and smell fresh. Choose a retailer that has a good turnover of spices, and buy in small quantities because the flavor diminishes over time. If you have specific storage containers for your spices make sure they can be easily washed and dried, and avoid buying replacements in glass containers because they tend to be more expensive and less environmentally friendly.

Also, store spices in airtight containers in a cool, dry, dark place because air and light destroy the flavor and color.

Whole spices can be used for some recipes, but for others they need to be crushed or ground. The best way to do this is either manually with a pestle and mortar, or electrically with a coffee or spice grinder. Make sure that the pestle fits snugly into the mortar, using a heavy, not lightweight, kind. If you use a regular coffee grinder, you will need to wipe it thoroughly before and after grinding spices in order to avoid tainting the coffee or the spices. Once you get the "spice bug" you may want a grinder specifically designated to the purpose.

Prior to grinding whole spices, you'll need to dry-roast them to bring out the mellowness and subtleties of the different flavors. Put them in a heavy-based skillet and place over a low heat. Move the spices around the skillet and heat for about 5 minutes until you can detect the strong aroma. Don't burn them, and allow to cool completely before grinding.

Grind spices in small quantities only (one or two tablespoons), or in a specific amount for your chosen purpose. Once ground, the seeds should be put through a coarse strainer to remove any stalks, husks, or foreign matter, such as small stones. Keep the spices separately in airtight glass jars in a cool, dark place, and only mix combinations together in quantities that you can use in a week or two at the most. Spice combinations (see pages 152–155) will lose their potency quite quickly after that.

SOME SPECIAL SPICES

Within the enormous world of spices, there are common types that need specific preparation:

Chili (*Capsicum frutescens*)

When buying fresh chilies, look for firm, shiny specimens with good color. They should be dry and heavy, and not limp, dull, or discolored. Store loose in the refrigerator for about two weeks. Chili juices can be an irritant to the skin, particularly of the hot chili varieties, so take extra care. Ideally it is best to wear thin, latex gloves to avoid getting any juice on the skin.

After washing and drying, slice down the length of the chili and carefully slice out the seeds and membrane by running the tip of a small knife beneath them. If the chili is small and fiddly, it is often easier to gently scrape out the seeds and membrane. Rinse under water to remove any stray seeds and then chop or slice, depending on the recipe. Rinse your hands in cold running water, and immediately wash the knife and board thoroughly. To remove the skin of the chili, lightly broil it, drop the chili into a plastic bag and the skin will peel off easily and safely.

The heat of the chilies is in the membrane and not the seeds, so make sure you remove all the membrane before use. Dried chilies should be lightly roasted and then soaked in hot water for about 10 minutes to rehydrate them. You may need to remove their seeds.

Note: Never rub your eyes or face when handling chilies in any form—the oil they contain is an irritant and will burn. If you do get any oil on your skin, wash it off with very large amounts of cold milk or soap and water. If you get any in your eyes, flush with lots of cool water.

Ginger (*Zingiber officinale*) and galangal (*Alpinia*)

Fresh gingerroot should feel firm, and the flesh should not be too fibrous. It will keep in the refrigerator for about two weeks. The buff-colored skin should be peeled with a vegetable peeler or small knife. Either chop fine using a knife, or shred using a bamboo grater. Galangal should also be peeled before using. The dried ginger bulb can be shredded directly into recipes or ground like other spices.

Lemongrass (*Cymbopogon citratus*)

Choose firm, long, fresh green stalks with a pale bulb. Trim the root end away, and strip off the outer leaves. Depending on the recipe, the stalks can either be used whole to infuse a dish and then discarded, or stripped down to the bulb and chopped fine, being added directly to the dish.

Nutmeg (*Myristica fragrans*)

Nutmeg is large enough to grate directly into a dish. Either use a small nutmeg grater, or the fine grating panel on a conventional grater.

Bell pepper (*Capsicum*)

When buying bell peppers look for smooth, firm skins and a good color. There shouldn't be any softness or discoloration. Peppers will keep in the refrigerator for three or four days, and in a cool pantry for two or three days. To prepare a pepper, wash and pat dry. Using a sharp knife, run the tip in a neat circle around the stalk, cutting through the flesh, and pull out the stalk. Slice down the middle of the pepper and scoop out the pale seeds. Slice out any of the central, paler membranes that run down the length of the pepper. To freeze, slice lengthwise and remove the seeds and membranes. Blanch them for two minutes. Cool under cold running water for two minutes and then drain and freeze for up to 12 months. When you want to use them, you can add the frozen slices to any recipe. If you prefer pepper halves, blanch them for three minutes and defrost for an hour before using.

THE SPICE DIRECTORY

The following pages offer a comprehensive photographic reference of both common spices—such as ginger, cinnamon, and pepper—and lesser-known spices—such as zedoary, grains of paradise, and quassia.

The spice directory shows the many different forms in which the spices are available—fresh, dried, or ground—and, in many cases, shows the spice growing in its native habitat.

There are spices to improve the dullest cooking, spices to blend, and spices that you'll never have used before. For each entry you'll find culinary uses, characteristics, tips, and a brief history of each spice and its origins. Sprinkled throughout the directory are delicious healthy recipes, both classic and modern, encouraging you to experiment with some new taste combinations.

Also included in each entry is information about the traditional medicinal uses of spices but, remember, you should refer any ailment or condition to a qualified medical physician before attempting to treat anything yourself at home.

SPICES BY COMMON NAME

GRAINS OF PARADISE
Amomum melegueta

Originally from western Africa, grains of paradise are widely used in both African and Caribbean cooking. Few outside these regions may have heard of them, but they are widely regarded as an aphrodisiac.

Grains of paradise, also known as melegueta pepper or Guinea grains, were certainly known and used in ancient Rome, and in medieval Europe. However in eighteenth-century Britain they were banned by King George III who believed that hot spices upset the body's natural balance of humors and were therefore bad for your health.

The seeds and rhizomes of the grains of paradise plant are thought to have stimulant and diuretic properties, and are often used in West African herbal medicines.

Description and parts used

The tree grows about 8 ft. (2.5m) high and is related to both ginger and cardamom. It produces orchid-like, trumpet-shaped flowers in yellow or pink with a yellow flash, which in turn produce brilliant scarlet fruits. They produce the tiny brown seeds of grains of paradise that are very unusual, being shaped like a blunt pyramid.

❦ CULINARY USES ❦

Because the flavor of grains of paradise is hot, spicy, and aromatic, they can be used to flavor any dishes in which you would normally use black pepper. They are certainly a popular seasoning in West Africa and in Morocco where they are one of the components of *ras el-hanout*, a locally used spice mix. Buy the whole seeds from a West Indian or African grocery store, and grind them yourself. They can also be ground with ginger to make an unusual spicy condiment.

You can also add grains of paradise to mulled wine for a warming "kick" or use in slow-cooked winter meat casseroles. Season meat marinades with the grains prior to barbecuing, or add to a tomato sauce for a peppery edge to serve with broiled meat or chicken.

GALANGAL
Alpinia genus

*Also known as Siamese ginger, the most well-known varieties
of galangal are* A. galangal *(greater galangal)
and* A. officinarum *(lesser galangal).*

Known by the Arab world in the ninth century, galangal was introduced to Europe by returning crusaders in the thirteenth century. In medieval times it was used in cooking and as an ingredient in perfume, but it fell out of favor by the eighteenth century. Galangal has an aromatic, pepper-ginger flavor, while the lesser variety is more pungent with a hint of eucalyptus. Medicinally, it makes a warming digestive and is used to treat gastric upsets.

Description and parts used

Greater galangal grows to about 10 ft. (3m) tall, with roots more than 3 ft. (90cm) long. The rhizomes have an orange-red skin and pale flesh. Lesser galangal grows only to around 5 ft. (1.5m) tall and has brown-skinned rhizomes with orange flesh. Galangal rhizomes are harvested in autumn when they are lifted, cleaned, and processed in a similar way to ginger and turmeric.

❦ CULINARY USES ❦

Greater galangal is the mildest and most most widely used variety of galangal. It can be bought as fresh root, dried root, or dried, ground powder. It is popular in Thailand, Malaysia, and Indonesia and is an essential component of Thai curry pastes, casseroles, and curries. Because it is subtler than lesser galangal, and has a more delicate flavor, it is suitable for people who prefer a mild curry. Sometimes the root is sliced as a garnish or used to season bread. The powdered root can be used in any dish in which you might traditionally use fresh ginger.

Lesser galangal is used in the manufacture of some bitters and liqueurs, and to flavor beers in Scandinavia and Russia. To store, wrap it in plastic wrap and keep in the pantry or refrigerator for up to a week.

DILL SEED
Anethum graveolens

*A familiar and much-loved herb, dill is also grown for its seeds that
are quite strong tasting, pungent and warming,
with a taste similar to caraway.*

Native to southwest and central Asia, the dill plant produces tiny, aromatic, yellow flowers that turn to fruit. If they are left to mature, the harvesting can begin when they turn yellow-brown at the end of summer. This is often carried out early in the morning when there is still dew on the plant. The seeds are then threshed and dried.

Because the flavor lingers in the mouth, the seeds can be used as a breath freshener. Like dill weed (see page 24), the seeds can be used as a digestive aid.

Description and parts used
The seeds are mid-brown with a lighter rim, and are oval, ribbed, curved, and flattish in shape. They are tiny—approximately 10,000 of them will weigh just 1oz (25g).

They can be used in the kitchen either whole or crushed, and the oil can be extracted and used as a flavoring.

❦ CULINARY USES ❦

Dill seed is a popular spice in Scandinavia where the seeds are used to flavor breads, potato dishes, and fish and shellfish. The French also are fond of dill, using the seeds in cakes and pastries. You can also use them as a pickling spice for vinegars when preserving vegetables, or add to marinades for fish, chicken, or pork.

Sprinkle lightly over freshly cooked vegetables—especially fava beans, stewed lentils, or other pulses. Alternatively, try using it as a light garnish sprinkled over creamy vegetable soups. Liven up plain freshly cooked pasta by tossing in a little sour cream and a few dill seeds. Serve with sausages or broiled pork, or add a few crushed seeds to rice and serve with rich oily fish, such as broiled salmon.

CELERY SEED
Apium graveolens

An excellent all-purpose ingredient that'll perk up a wide range of salads, soups, and casseroles, and help improve your health.

From the little wild celery, known as "smallage," that grows wild throughout Europe in river estuaries and salt marshes, we get the cultivated celery seed. Smallage, once used as a medicine, would taste very bitter to the modern palate but the Romans used it as a flavoring. Stems and leaves of cultivated celery are used as a vegetable, raw in salads, braised as a vegetable, or cooked as a base flavoring, like onions. The seeds of the wild celery are used as a spice, and are warming and aromatic but quite bitter. Eating the seeds of raw, cultivated celery is said to lower blood pressure, to stimulate digestion, and to treat rheumatism.

Description and parts used

The seeds come from the second year's growth of the plant. Once the seed heads form, they are dried and the seeds are shaken out. Celery seeds are tiny, oval, and mid-dark brown with lighter ridges.

❦ CULINARY USES ❦

The seed of the wild celery plant is quite strong and bitter, so you need very small quantities. It can be used whole to flavor soups and casseroles, or ground and mixed with salt and used as a condiment. It makes an interesting flavoring for ketchups and sauces, and is very good with tomatoes. Try adding to bread dough, or use with cheese and egg dishes. The seed also gives a warming note to a salad dressing, and is good for a winter coleslaw. Celery salt, a salt-based seasoning flavored with the essential oil, is more widely available but soon develops a stale taste.

Caution: The seeds sold for cultivation should not be used for medicinal purposes because they may well have been treated with fungicides.

MUSTARD
Brassica

*Mustard is easy to grow and thrives in temperate climates.
It is one of the most common and widely used of all
spices, and has an unmistakable flavor.*

Mustard has been used for so long that its origins are lost, but it probably came from the eastern Mediterranean, where it grows as a weed and is used for feeding horses. The Romans were probably the first to recognize its importance in cooking, and they spread it to all the parts of their empire.

The name comes from two Latin words, *mustum* and *ardere*, meaning "fresh grape juice," and "to burn." This refers to the method originally used to process mustard—mixing it with grape juice at a burning hot temperature.

Description and parts used

Mustard is a spindly plant that grows around 3 ft. tall, with bright yellow flowers. The seeds are usually brown or reddish.

B. nigra is black mustard, and is now only grown in peasant economies. It has been replaced in large-scale farming by brown mustard (*B. juncea*).

☙ CULINARY USES ☙

Mustard powder should always be mixed with cold liquid—grape juice, vinegar, or water; if it is mixed with hot liquid, the heat is eliminated. The seeds are ground and used as a fiery spice for making a condiment, to accompany many dishes from cold and hot meats to cheeses, and to include in sauces for hot dishes and dressings for salads. You can also use it to add piquancy to cheese sauces and mayonnaise. Whole seeds are used in curries and for pickling, and are best dry roasted first. The seeds can also be sprouted to make a salad ingredient.

Caution: Mustard contains substances that can irritate the delicate membranes of the nose and mouth and is also a skin irritant; in large doses, it can cause vomiting.

MUSTARD VARIETIES

There are two basic types of mustard seed: brown and white. The brown mustard seeds are more aromatic and tasty, while the white ones are larger and hotter. All mustard blends are combinations of these two types of seeds.

AMERICAN—made from powdered white seeds and flour, vinegar, and coloring. It is excellent with hot dogs and hamburgers.

BORDEAUX—made with whole seeds and mixed with vinegar, sugar, and tarragon. It is used as an accompaniment to cold meats.

COARSE GRAIN—a type of Moutarde de Meaux (see opposite), which has had white wine added to it. Quite hot.

DIJON—made from brown seeds that are husked and ground, and mixed with verjuice (unripe grape juice). Used to flavor mayonnaise and hot or cold sauces.

DUSSELDORF—a type of German mustard (see opposite), without the spices and caramel. It is not nearly as mild as German mustard and is best eaten with spicy food.

ENGLISH—made from a combination of both white and brown seeds (roughly 20 percent white seeds and 80 percent brown seeds), which are mixed with flour and turmeric. It is often sold as a dry, bright yellow powder. Cold water is added to it to make a traditional hot English mustard. It should always be allowed to stand for 10 minutes to allow the flavor to develop fully.

A traditional accompaniment to meat dishes, such as roast beef or cold ham.

ENGLISH WHOLE GRAIN—a pungent, hot mustard made from whole white seeds with white wine, black pepper (see page 140), and allspice (see page 136).

FLORIDA—a Bordeaux mustard made with wine, not vinegar, from the Champagne region.

GERMAN—very similar to Bordeaux mustard, but it is usually flavored with spices, herbs, and caramel that tends to make it darker and tastier. Good with cold meats and sausages.

GREEN PEPPERCORN—made with Dijon mustard with crushed green peppercorns added to it; popular in Burgundy, where it is eaten with broiled meat. Quite hot and spicy.

MOUTARDE DE MEAUX—a Dijon mustard made with whole brown seeds. Pleasantly hot and best eaten with foods that are not so spicy.

TARRAGON—a Bordeaux-type mustard flavored with tarragon. It is quite mild and is excellent with other spicy foods.

WHITE WINE—a Dijon mustard made with white wine. Quite hot, it is used for flavoring sauces.

CAPERS
Capparis spinosa

In southern Europe, the pickled caper has been used as a condiment for at least the last 2,000 years. The characteristic flavor comes from the capric acid that develops when the flower buds are pickled in vinegar, and turn olive green.

The caper is the flower bud of a Mediterranean shrub that grows in France, Spain, and Italy. It is used widely in North African cooking and throughout the whole of the Mediterranean, especially in Sardinia. Increasingly used in the West, capers add an unexpected, refreshing taste.

Medicinally capers can also be used to aid digestion and increase the appetite, and to induce a general feeling of well-being and vitality. The flower buds can be infused in a tea to ease coughs.

Description and parts used

Capers grow wild throughout the Mediterranean, where they are regarded as weeds. The plant has thick, shiny leaves, long prickles and short-lived flowers that have purple stamens and fringed white petals streaked pale pink. As well as the flower buds, the plant bears fruit that is also pickled.

❦ CULINARY USES ❦

Whole caper buds are available pickled in brine or vinegar, or packed in salt. They are best drained and rinsed before using. Add to casseroles and lamb dishes, as well as to tartare sauce. They are a good complement to smoked meat or fish, and can also be added to parsley and sprinkled over beef, or used to top a tomato-based or fish-topped pizza. They are also an essential ingredient in tapenade—an olive paste made in the Mediterranean (see recipe opposite)—and in caponata, a Sardinian salad of eggplants and tuna.

Capers should be kept in a non-corrosive glass jar. Keep them immersed in the bottling liquid or under a layer of salt to prevent them drying out and, once opened, store in the refrigerator.

BLACK OLIVE TAPENADE

This flavorful spread is delicious on crisp, thin little toasts, or spread onto crusty baguettes for a heartier bite. Serves 4.

INGREDIENTS

1 onion, chopped
4 tbsp olive oil
3 ripe fresh tomatoes, chopped
1 lb fresh mushrooms, finely chopped
2 sprigs fresh thyme
Broth or white wine
2 tbsp capers in brine, drained
3 garlic cloves, chopped
25 black olives, pitted and chopped
Ground black pepper, to taste

METHOD

1 Lightly sauté the onion in olive oil until softened and golden brown, about 10 to 15 minutes.

2 Add the tomatoes, and continue cooking until the mixture becomes pastelike. Add the mushrooms and thyme, and cook gently for about 20 minutes, stirring and turning occasionally, until the mushrooms are very soft and tender. If the mixture becomes too dry, add some broth or white wine.

3 When the mixture has thickened, remove from the heat, and stir in the capers, garlic, and olives. Mix well and season with pepper. Allow to cool to room temperature.

BELL PEPPERS
Capsicum annuum

Bell peppers originally came from tropical America but are now cultivated the world over in warm climates. They are milder and more flavorful than chilies, and can be eaten raw without any ill effects or burning sensations.

The taste of these peppers, also known as pimentos and capsicums, is fresh and juicy, and they have a clear, tangy texture. They are extremely versatile in the kitchen.

Medicinally, bell peppers are said to have revitalizing and antiseptic qualities, and are used to stimulate the digestive system. The peppers also contain large amounts of vitamin C, and their sweet flavor and cheery color make them a real feelgood food.

Description and parts used

Sweet bell peppers grow on bushes about 3 ft. tall, with white flowers. The fruits start off green and slowly turn red, orange, or yellow as they mature.

Red and orange varieties are the sweetest, while the immature green ones can be used in the same way but may be quite bitter. The dried and ground flesh of red peppers is made into paprika (see page 104).

❦ CULINARY USES ❦

Bell peppers can be sliced and eaten raw on their own or in salads, but the seeds should be removed before using. They are also excellent pickled or in relishes. They preserve well when roasted or broiled, then packed in olive oil, and seasoned with garlic and herbs. They are a major ingredient in many famous vegetable dishes, such as French ratatouille, Middle Eastern fattoush (see opposite), and the summery Spanish soup, gazpacho.

Whole peppers make good baking containers for meat, rice, or couscous stuffings. Sliced peppers make a delicious addition to goat's-cheese quiches and flans. Try slow-cooking slices of bell pepper, then chop and add to an omelet or scrambled egg. For specific preparation and storage, see page 87.

FATTOUSH

This popular Lebanese salsa has pieces of crisply toasted pita bread
added just before serving. This allows the pita to soak up some
bell-pepper juices without becoming soggy. Serves 4 to 6.

INGREDIENTS

1 cucumber, diced
2 medium red bell peppers, cored, deseeded,
 and diced
4 ripe tomatoes, diced
$^1/_2$ cup black olives
Bunch of scallions, thickly sliced on the diagonal
2 tbsp chopped fresh flat-leaf parsley
2 pita breads, toasted until crisp and golden
Juice of $^1/_2$ lemon
3 tbsp olive oil
Salt and freshly ground black pepper

METHOD

1 Toss together the cucumber, peppers,
 tomatoes, olives, scallions, and parsley in
 a large bowl.
2 Tear the toasted pitas into bite-sized pieces
 and add to the cucumber-pepper mixture.
3 Whisk together the lemon juice, olive oil, and
 plenty of seasoning.
4 Pour over the salad, toss well together, and
 serve immediately.

CHILI
Capsicum frutescens

*They tend to come with a strong, hidden warning—"beware heat"—
but there are actually many kinds that are quite mild,
and some that are even fruity.*

Although related to bell peppers, there is a considerable difference in size, color, shape, and strength of flavor. There is an old saying that the smaller they are, the hotter they are, but be careful because some of the larger ones are very hot indeed. There is evidence that chilies have been grown and used in Central and South America for at least 9,000 years, but they were taken to Europe by Spanish explorers. Medicinally, chilies have a strong stimulant effect. They make a warming treatment for colds and have good antibacterial properties.

Description and parts uses

Chilies can be grown in temperate climates, but they need artificial heat. They grow to about 6½ ft. tall, with the fleshy fruit pods containing white seeds. Color is dependent on variety. Chilies are dried whole, or are dried and ground to make chili powder and cayenne pepper (see page 102).

❦ CULINARY USES ❦

Care must be taken when preparing and using fresh chilies—see page 86 for specific instructions. In the tropics they are used to enhance bland, starchy staple foods, such as grains, yuca, and peas and beans. Chilies provide heat to curries, spice blends, pastes, and relishes, and to sauces and condiments. Use cautiously to avoid overpowering a dish. Chop finely and add at the beginning of cooking to add spiciness to robust meat dishes, or to vegetable and bean casseroles and soups. For more delicate ingredients, choose a mild variety or pierce a whole chili and add to the cooking liquid to give a gentler flavor. Discard before serving.

Caution: Taken in excess, chilies may damage the mucous membranes, and cause digestive and renal problems.

CHILI VARIETIES

Today there are more than 150 varieties of chilies, and they are grown
principally in Mexico, California, Texas, New Mexico, Arizona, Thailand,
India, Africa, and Asia. They come in all shapes, sizes and colors and
can be bought fresh or canned, dried, pickled in brine, or powdered. Here
are some of the most popular, each graded on a scale
from 1 (mildest) to 5 (hottest).

ANAHEIM – Also known as the Californian chili or
New Mexican chili, anaheim is about 6 in. long
and either bright green or, when fully ripened,
red. It looks a little like a bell pepper. When
it is dried and powdered, it is sold as "Colorado
chili powder."
Scores a mild 1.

BIRD'S EYE – Tiny and extremely hot, bird's eye
is popular in eastern Asian cooking.
Scores a very hot 5.

HABANERO – One of the hottest chilies, habañero
grows in Central America and the Caribbean. It
varies from red to green to purple, and is 2 in.
long. When ripe, it is said to have a fruity,
tropical flavor—if you can get through the heat.
Scores a distinct 5 plus.

JALAPEÑO – Commonly used, jalapeño grows in
Mexico and across southwestern U.S. Juicy and
plump, about 2–3 in. long. Can be red or

green—but the red are more flavorful. Dried and
smoked, it is known as a chipotle chile.
Scores a medium 2–3.

MALAGUETTA – A fiery, tiny, thin chili from Brazil.
It is used green (unripe) or red (ripe).
Scores a very hot 5.

POBLANO – Green or red chili from Mexico and
California. Grows to 4–6 in. with thickish flesh.
Dried it is known as an ancho chile.
Scores a quite mild 2.

SCOTCH BONNET – Grows in the Caribbean, this is
1 in. long. Often described as having a smoky,
fruity flavor, but the heat may not allow you
taste much of this.
Scores a scorching 5 plus.

SERRANO – A very thin chili, red or green and
2 in. long with a clean, sweet, flavorful taste.
Scores a hot 4.

CAYENNE PEPPER
Capsicum longum

If you dry fresh red chilies and grind them up, you have the makings of cayenne pepper. Manufactured cayenne pepper is a pungent, finely ground orange-red spice made from a blend of small, ripe chilies of various origins.

Apparently, cayenne pepper was used by the cooks of chuck wagons on the cattle drives across the Texas plains to flavor some pretty unsavory food, such as rattlesnake. A lot of the cooks sowed cayenne and other seeds along the cattle trails so that they could have fresh herbs and spices in later years. Cayenne is used all over the world; it is known as *lal mirch* in India, and *pisihui* in southeast Asia.

The warming properties of cayenne means that it is added to ointments for the treatment of neuralgia, chilblains, and lumbago.

Description and parts used

Traditionally, the cayenne chili, as its Latin name suggests, is about 2–4 in. long. It is thin, tapering to a point, and it is very hot. The chilies are harvested for use when bright red and ripe, and are grown and dried in Louisiana and Mexico.

🌶 CULINARY USES 🌶

The versatile cayenne pepper can be used in hot dishes, such as chili con carne, or in mild dishes, such as smoked salmon risotto (see recipe opposite). Cayenne can be added to any red meat or game dish, or a hearty bean casserole, to which you want to add heat without extra flavor.

You can also add the merest pinch of cayenne to cheese sauces and mayonnaise salad dressing (instead of mustard) to give them a bit of zip and added color. Sprinkle a little over a fresh crab or lobster salad, or on top of a classic prawn cocktail. Add a little to an egg mayonnaise sandwich filling, or on top of a cheese quiche. Cayenne will liven up a thick winter soup and be very warming on a cold day.

SMOKED SALMON RISOTTO

Smoked salmon is enhanced by the anise seed flavor of dill weed, colored by cayenne pepper. Feathery dill fronds make a glamorous garnish. Serves 4.

INGREDIENTS

3¼ cups fish broth
1¼ cups dry white wine
4 tbsp butter
2 tbsp lemon juice
1 red onion, finely chopped
2 garlic cloves, minced
2 cups arborio rice
Salt and freshly ground black pepper
1 tsp cayenne pepper
4 tbsp chopped fresh dill weed
10 oz smoked salmon, cut into strips
²/₃ cup light cream
Sprigs fresh dill weed, to garnish

METHOD

1 Pour the broth and wine into a pan and bring to a boil. Reduce the heat to a gentle simmer.

2 Meanwhile, melt the butter in a large skillet and add the lemon juice. Gently fry the onion and garlic, stirring, until the onion has softened but not browned. Stir in the rice and cook gently, stirring, for 2 minutes until the rice is well-coated in butter.

3 Add a ladleful of the broth and wine mixture to the rice and cook gently, stirring, until absorbed. Continue adding the broth mixture until half of the broth has been used. Season well and add the cayenne pepper.

4 Continue adding broth for a further 20 minutes. Stir in the dill weed, salmon, and cream, and continue cooking, adding broth for a further 5 minutes until the risotto is thick but not sticky.

5 Serve in a bowl, garnished with dill weed.

PAPRIKA
Capsicum tetragonum

Bright red paprika is made from red bell peppers, and has more flavor and less heat than cayenne pepper. It is the traditional ingredient in Hungarian goulash (beef casserole).

The Turkish masters of the Ottoman Empire introduced paprika to Hungary where it is now the national spice of the country, being used in many meat dishes and treated with almost religious fervor.

In 1926 a Hungarian chemist first isolated vitamin C from paprika, and together with the spice's warming qualities it can be regarded as the perfect antidote to winter.

Description and parts used

Paprika is made only from red bell peppers (see page 98) that are dried and ground, but most commercially produced paprika has little in the way of heat.

Its bitterness depends on how much seed is used—ideally only the dried fruit should be used to make good paprika, and the lighter in color the red peppers, the hotter the spice. Paprika is also available smoked.

❦ CULINARY USES ❦

If you don't like the heat of chilies, this is the spice to choose instead of cayenne. Paprika is used throughout Europe, especially in Portugal and Spain, but the Hungarians use paprika the most to flavor and color many dishes including soups, vegetables, chicken, fish, and meat (see opposite). It is also used as an ingredient in Cajun seasoning (see page 153).

You can also use it to add a splash of color to a garnish on a canapé, or to light colored soups, egg dishes, and vegetables. Use to color and flavor sauces for shellfish and chicken, or add to dressings for salads. Paprika doesn't keep very well—it quickly loses color and flavor—and should be bought in small quantities.

HUMMUS WITH PAPRIKA

This Middle Eastern dip, traditionally garnished with paprika, is
delicious with fresh bread or crudites. Makes about 1 cup.

INGREDIENTS

7 oz can garbanzo beans
3 plump cloves garlic, peeled
$^{1}/_{2}$ cup tahini paste
$^{1}/_{3}$ cup olive oil
Salt and freshly ground black pepper
Juice of $^{1}/_{2}$ a lemon
Sprinkling of ground paprika

METHOD

1 Drain the beans, reserving the liquid. Place the
  beans in a blender with the garlic, tahini, and
  olive oil and blend until smooth.

2 Add as much liquid reserved from the beans
  as necessary to make a thick paste. Season
  well with the salt and pepper, then add lemon
  juice to taste.

3 Spoon the hummus into a serving dish and
  chill lightly. Sprinkle with ground paprika just
  before serving.

CARAWAY
Carum carvi

Caraway seeds have a pungent aroma with a warming, almost citrus flavor. The seeds can be chewed for relief of indigestion and stomach cramps.

You would not think that such a small, nondescript plant could have so many uses or be so highly prized as a charm against witchcraft and demons. It was once believed that anything containing caraway could not be stolen, and was fed to pigeons to stop them straying. It was even thought that if a wife placed a few seeds in her husband's pockets, he could not have his heart stolen away. Today it's highly valued for its marvelous flavor.

Description and parts used

Caraway grows wild throughout Europe and Asia and has now been naturalized in the U.S. and Canada, and is cultivated in the Netherlands and Russia on a large scale. It grows only about 8 in. tall, with white or pink flowers. The stems are cut once the fruit ripens, and the seeds are then threshed and dried. The seeds are primarily used, but the leaves can be eaten fresh in salads or cooked in casseroles.

❦ CULINARY USES ❦

The seeds of caraway are used whole or lightly crushed to flavor caraway candy, and the oil of the caraway is used to make liqueurs, such as the northern European favorite, kümmel. The ground seeds of caraway are used in curry powder, as well as in flavoring for cakes, breads, and cookies. Caraway is very popular in Jewish, German, and Scandinavian cooking, being used to flavor the sauerkraut, cabbage, soups, and sausages so popular in these cuisines. The root can be boiled in the same way as a root vegetable and tastes similar to parsnip.

Gently fried seeds are delicious with apples and cheese—and they can even dipped in sugar to make sugar plums. A traditional seed cake always includes a generous amount of caraway seeds in the cake batter.

CASSIA
Cinnamomum cassia

It is one of the oldest spices to be used as a medicine, and was first used in China in 2,700 BC and in Egypt in 1,600 BC. In the West, cassia is a major ingredient in cold remedies, and it is also used to treat digestive problems.

A native to Assam and northern Burma, the bark of cassia (also known as Chinese cinnamon) is a form of cinnamon. In many countries the names cassia and cinnamon are used interchangeably; in the U.S. it is used and sold simply as cinnamon.

Cassia's taste is regarded as less delicate than that of cinnamon and its texture thicker and rougher—in fact, is rather regarded as a poor substitute to cinnamon.

Description and parts used

Cassia grows in most Asian countries, and the bark is dried in quills for powdering and for using in infusions and tinctures. The twigs and leaves are distilled for their oil which contains around 85 percent cinnamaldehyde, an important product in the pharmaceutical, cosmetic, and food industries. The clovelike buds are harvested and dried for use as a flavoring in the food industry.

☙ CULINARY USES ☙

Although the spices are closely related, the taste of cassia and cinnamon does differ. Cassia has a stronger taste than cinnamon, but some people find that it tastes sweeter and prefer it for flavoring mulled wine and desserts. In the U.S. cassia is used as a sweet spice for flavoring cakes, cookies, and pastries, while in Asia it is used as a flavoring for curries and meat dishes.

Cassia is one of the five ingredients in Chinese five-spice (see page 152)—a mixture used to flavor roasted meats, poultry, and marinades. Try adding to stewing apples or a dried-fruit compote. In India, cassia is often added to a rice pilaf, and is excellent added to couscous and lentil dishes. The flowers and dried bark are attractive and can be used in potpourri.

CINNAMON
Cinnamomum zeylanicum

Cinnamon has a delicious sweet flavor that gives a warming sensation, and a woody aroma. Medicinally, it is a strong stimulant for the glandular system, and helps relieve the symptoms of colds and flu.

Since ancient times, the fragrant, dried inner bark of the cinnamon tree has been a valued spice. The Phoenician traders probably brought it to the Middle East. Since the ninth century it has been widely used in Europe, and most of the cinnamon that is used today comes from Sri Lanka.

Description and parts used

In its native habitat this bushy, evergreen tree can grow to 30 ft. The deeply veined fragrant leaves are long and dark green with lighter undersides. The small yellow flowers turn into dark purple berries. The bark is the part that is used in the kitchen. It is peeled off and left to dry for a day, then the outer bark is stripped away, and the inner bark rolls itself into tight sticks as it dries. The highest quality cinnamon is made from the thinnest bark, which has the best taste and fragrance.

🌿 CULINARY USES 🌿

In the Middle East, cinnamon is often added to lamb casseroles and is ground and sprinkled over couscous dishes. It is added to sweet syrups, which are poured over nutty pastries and desserts. For spicing hot drinks such as mulled wine, whole cinnamon sticks are used, and the sticks make good stirrers to enhance a spicy drink. Add a stick to stewed fruit like apple or pear. Cinnamon is also very good with chocolate; add a pinch to bring out the richness. For a simple treat, sprinkle ground cinnamon and brown sugar over hot buttered toast, and top with sliced banana.

Cinnamon is best when bought in sticks, but it can also be bought ground. Ground cinnamon actually tastes stronger, but it loses its flavor and aroma quickly.

APPLE AND CINNAMON MUFFINS

The apple and cinnamon in these muffins complement each other without competing for attention. Makes 6.

INGREDIENTS

2 ³/₄ cups all-purpose flour
1 ¹/₄ cups superfine sugar
4 tsp baking powder
2 tsp ground cinnamon
4 tbsp vegetable oil
¹/₄ cup butter, melted
2 lightly beaten eggs
³/₄ cup buttermilk
2 small apples, peeled, cored, and finely diced

METHOD

1 Preheat the oven to 350°F. Grease a 12-cup muffin pan. In a medium bowl, combine the flour, sugar, baking powder, and cinnamon. Set aside.

2 In a large bowl, beat the oil, butter, eggs, and buttermilk with an electric mixer until well combined. Add the flour mixture and beat until nearly combined. Stir in the apples. Do not overmix. Spoon the mixture into the prepared pan.

3 Bake for 20 minutes. Remove pan from the oven and cool for 5 minutes. Then remove the muffins and cool on a rack.

4 Store in an airtight container for up to 2 days, or freeze for up to 3 months.

KAFFIR LIME

Citrus hystrix

In Sri Lanka and Indonesia, kaffir lime is used as an insect repellent and as a cleansing hair rinse. It can be grown as a conservatory plant and the leaves can be picked year-round for use in the kitchen.

Citrus hystrix is a small tree from southeast Asia, the fruit being commonly used in Thai and Indonesian cooking. It isn't strictly a lime, but a sub-species of the citrus family called *paepeda*. The lime green fruits aren't sweet enough to eat on their own, but the bitter rind and very acidic juice are used in cooking. Kaffir lime leaves can be used in the same way as bay leaves, and give an aromatic lemon-verbena flavor to many dishes.

Description and parts used

The fruits are dumpy and pear-shaped, covered in bumpy, wrinkled skin that can be shredded like other citrus fruit. Inside, the flesh looks like a lime. The leaves are rich green in color, smooth, and leathery like bay leaves, but have an unusual double form as if two leaves have grown end to end.

CULINARY USES

Kaffir lime gives a fragrant, lemon flavor to meat dishes, such as pork, chicken, and fish. The leaves are often infused in coconut milk and used as a base for Thai curries, or are added to broths, soups, and rice dishes.

Try adding to milk or cream and infusing to make sauces or a lemony rice dessert. Or try infusing a sugar syrup with rind, leaf, and juice, and pour over other citrus fruit. Like bay leaves, you should discard the leaves of kaffir lime before serving.

The rind is added to Thai curry pastes and the leaves are added to Indonesian spice mixes, such as *sambal badjak*. The leaves can be used fresh or dried—although the latter is much less fragrant.

CORIANDER
Coriandrum sativum

*Coriander seeds have a pungent
flavor and are traditionally used to spice up a wide
range of dishes, from meat to fish.*

Cilantro is a small, annual herb that grows wild throughout the Mediterranean. The name cilantro is used to refer to the leaves of the plant (see page 36) while coriander refers to the seeds. The ripened, round, light brown seeds do taste deliciously sweet and have a slightly warming, citrus taste. Moroccan seeds are most commonly available, but Indian seed has a slightly sweeter flavor and is lighter in color. The seeds can be used to treat digestive problems.

Origins and characteristics

Cilantro grown in warmer climates has much larger fruit than that grown in more temperate regions. If the seeds are harvested in late summer and dried, they keep their scent over a long period. The seeds are also available ground. In Asia, especially China, the leaves are used to flavor many dishes. In Thailand the root is cooked with garlic and used in curry pastes.

❧ CULINARY USES ❧

Coriander seeds can be used for cooking fish, poultry, and vegetable dishes. They can also be added to bread and cake batters. The ground seeds can be added to sausages, curries, and rubbed on meat before roasting.

The seeds are frequently added to pickling liquid for preserving vegetables, and can be ground and mixed with other sweet spices when it's called dessert spice (or pumpkin pie spice) for flavoring fruit and rice desserts, cakes, and vanilla pie-filling.

Add a few lightly crushed seeds to fresh lemonade, or to hot toddies along with cinnamon. As with most ground spice, ground coriander is less sweet and loses its flavor more quickly than fresh crushed seeds.

SAFFRON
Crocus sativus

At various times, saffron has been more expensive than gold, and it still is the most expensive spice in the world. It's highly rated in the kitchen, where fortunately a little goes a long, long way.

Saffron is deep, dark orange-gold, and is made from the dried stigmas of a blue-flowered crocus, native to Turkey. Scores of stigmas (from about 200–500) are needed to make just $^3/_{100}$ oz, and the slender stigmas are so delicate they have to be handpicked. All these factors account for saffron's high value.

Luckily, very little of the spice is needed to impart its wonderful, slightly flowery, bitter taste and its rich, golden color in cooking. You can infuse saffron to make an herbal tea that is taken as a warming, soothing drink to clear the head.

Description and parts used

Saffron is available in threads or ground. Ideally, purchase threads because any artificial dying or coloring is easier to spot. Safflower (or "bastard saffron") stigmas are often passed off as saffron, but they are redder in color, spindlier, and have little or no flavor. Turmeric (see page 116) is also sold as saffron, but it is easy to spot because it has quite a different color and taste.

🐦 CULINARY USES 🐦

Used to flavor and color food since ancient times, saffron is an essential ingredient in paella, bouillabaisse, risotto alla Milanese (see recipe opposite), and, of course, saffron cakes. Saffron is good for flavoring shellfish and fish, and is a useful ingredient in creamy sauces. Saffron threads should be broken up and infused in a little hot water; the strained liquid is then added to the dish according to the recipe instructions. You can dry the threads in the oven first, and then crumble them into the recipe. The threads should be dark orange with no white streaks. Ground saffron should also be infused before it is used. A pinch is enough to flavor rice for four people.

Caution: Make sure only the stigmas from *Crocus sativus* are used—the unrelated plant, the autumn crocus (*Colchicum autumnal*), is very similar but poisonous.

RISOTTO ALLA MILANESE

This colorful and aromatic risotto has the added sweetness
of bell peppers and Marsala wine. Serves 4.

INGREDIENTS

6 medium bell peppers, 2 each of red, yellow,
  and green
4 tbsp Marsala wine
5 cups vegetable broth
2 tbsp olive oil
1 medium onion, chopped fine
14 oz arborio rice
Large pinch ground saffron
Salt and freshly ground black pepper

METHOD

1 Preheat the broiler to hot. Halve and seed the
  peppers and broil for 7 to 8 minutes, turning
  occasionally, until they are charred and
  softened. Peel off the charred skin, then slice

the peppers into strips. Place in a shallow
bowl and mix in the Marsala. Set aside.

2 Pour the broth into a saucepan, bring to a
  boil, and reduce to a simmer. Heat the oil in a
  large skillet and fry the onion until softened,
  but not browned. Stir in the rice until well
  coated in the onion mixture.

3 Add a ladleful of broth and cook, stirring,
  until absorbed. Continue adding the broth,
  ladle by ladle, until half the broth is used and
  the rice becomes creamy.

4 Sprinkle in the ground saffron and seasoning.
  Continue adding the broth until the rice is
  tender. This will take about 25 minutes.

5 Stir in the bell-pepper mixture and adjust the
  seasoning. Serve immediately.

CUMIN
Cuminum cyminum

An essential ingredient in Eastern cuisine, cumin adds a highly distinctive note to a wide range of recipes from curries to dips.

Cumin is a native of the Middle East. Its seedlike fruit produces a pungent, aromatic spice, similar to caraway. It also features in Greek and Turkish cooking. The ancient Romans used cumin as we use black pepper today, but it is probably best known for its role in Indian cuisine, especially curries and chicken roasted in a *tandoor* (clay oven). Medicinally, cumin is taken for minor digestive disorders, and is believed to settle stomach upsets.

Description and parts used

Cumin will grow in any warm, sunny position in rich, well-drained, sandy loam. It grows about 2 ft. tall, with very slender stems and tiny pink or white flowers. Indian cumin comes in two varieties: white (*safed*) and black (*kala*). The black variety has a more subtle flavor but is hard to find outside India. The fruits are picked before they are fully ripe and are left to dry. They are then used ground or whole.

❦ CULINARY USES ❦

Cumin is used in the popular spice blend garam masala (see page 153) and is an important ingredient of many North African couscous dishes—cracked wheat steamed and served with spicy meat, vegetables, chickpeas, and raisins.

Cumin is also used to flavor meats and cheeses. In Spain it is used in combination with saffron and cinnamon in casseroles, and in Texas is added to chili con carne. Roast the seeds and add to marinades for lamb or add to dressings and dips, such as hummus, or chopped cucumber, onion, and yogurt with fresh cilantro. Ground cumin doesn't store well, and should be bought in small quantities. Because whole seeds are difficult to grind finely with a mortar, buy both whole seeds and the ground powder.

SPICY GARLIC SHRIMP

Silky coconut milk combined with fiery spices livens up this shrimp dish.
Reduce or even remove the chili if a milder taste is desired. Serves 4.

INGREDIENTS

2 cups uncooked shrimp, peeled and deveined
2 large zucchini, cut into julienne strips
1 red chili, chopped fine
1 carrot, cut into julienne strips
1 red bell pepper, cut into julienne strips
2 tomatoes, deseeded and chopped
2 tbsp olive oil
1 tsp fresh gingerroot, shredded
4 cloves garlic, peeled and minced
Juice and zest of 1 medium lime
1 tsp ground turmeric
1 tsp ground coriander
1 tsp ground cumin
4 tbsp coconut milk
1 tbsp light soy sauce
8 oz dry egg noodles

METHOD

1 Rinse the shrimp under running water and
pat dry. Put in a shallow glass dish with the
vegetables. Combine the oil, ginger, garlic,
lime, spices, coconut milk, and soy sauce, and
pour over the vegetables. Cover and marinate
for 1 hour, turning occasionally.

2 Half-fill the base of a steamer with boiling
water. Place dampened waxed paper in the
steamer top and add the shrimp mixture.
Place over the steamer, cover with a tight-
fitting lid and steam for 10 minutes.

3 Put the noodles into the boiling water in the
steamer base and cook for 5 minutes or until
the noodles and shrimp are cooked.

4 Drain the noodles, top with the shrimp
mixture, garnish, and serve.

TURMERIC
Curcuma longa

Turmeric has been used in Asia for centuries as a dye and medicine. In some places, it is also believed to have magical powers and is worn as a protective charm to ward off evil spirits.

Turmeric is related to ginger and is also obtained from the rhizomes, which are harvested and processed, again, like ginger. It is a native of India where some 12,000 tons of it are produced annually, but it is now cultivated throughout the world, especially in China, Java, and Peru. Most of this is exported. Turmeric is always traded whole and ground by the importing country. The rhizomes are boiled, dried, peeled, and then ground to produce a bright yellow spice that is lightly aromatic, with a fresh peppery smell, and slightly pungent taste. Turmeric is a strong stimulant of the digestive and respiratory systems and also has anti-inflammatory and antiseptic properties.

Description and parts used
Turmeric grows about 2 ft. tall, with large, broad leaves and yellow flowers. Covered in rough, light brown skin, the rhizomes are a bright orange color inside.

❦ CULINARY USES ❦

Turmeric is one of the principal ingredients of curry powder (see page 153), and is widely used in Indian vegetarian cooking. It is also a popular ingredient for many south Asian recipes. Turmeric is often added to cooking rice to give it a delicate yellow color. Its name comes from the Arabic word *kurkum*, which means "saffron," but the two should not be confused (see page 112).

Turmeric is the flavoring used for Worcestershire sauce and piccalilli, the pickled vegetable relish. It is added to mustard and some cheeses to enhance the yellow color. Turmeric is almost always sold as a ground powder because the root is very hard to grind. Only small quantities should be bought because it loses its flavor, although not its color, very quickly.

ZEDOARY
Curcuma zedoaria

*Similar to ginger and often combined with pepper, cinnamon, and honey,
it is highly rated in the perfume industry for its musky undertones,
and in the kitchen for its flavor.*

The herb comes from southeast Asian subtropical rainforests. The rhizome is dried to provide a spice resembling ginger, and it has a resinous and slightly pungent flavor (reminiscent of rosemary). Zedoary was taken to Europe in the sixth century by Arabian traders as a medicine and perfume. Like galangal (see page 91), zedoary was very popular in medieval European kitchens, but is virtually unknown today in the West. The rhizomes are rich in starch, which is extracted and used in Indian cooking as a thickening agent, called *shoti*, which is similar to arrowroot. The starch is easy to digest and is given to the infirm and babies.

Description and parts used

The plant has large, broad, green leaves and bracts of red, green, or yellow flowers. It has a large, fleshy, yellow rhizome, fibrous in texture, which can be sliced, dried, and ground to make the spice.

❦ CULINARY USES ❦

In countries where the spice is grown, zedoary is used to flavor condiments and as an alternative to ginger or turmeric. In southern India, zedoary is used to flavor chicken and lamb dishes, as well as vegetables. In Java, Indonesia, the young shoots are eaten raw and have a flavor similar to lemongrass. They are also used to flavor fish, or are eaten in salads or as a vegetable on their own.

Zedoary is not widely known in Europe and North America where ginger can be used as a substitute, although it is worth remembering that the flavor of zedoary is not as bitter as ginger. (If substituting ginger for zedoary, you may need to use less ginger and adjust any sweetening ingredients in the recipe.)

LEMONGRASS
Cymbopogon citratus

*Lemongrass comes from southeast Asia and is a principal ingredient
in Thai, Malaysian, and Indonesian cooking and curries. The leaves,
when crushed, add a delightful fragrance to soaps and perfumes.*

Although lemongrass is a relatively new spice in Europe and North America, the increase in popularity of Thai and Indonesian cooking means it's now available in most supermarkets and greengrocers. Asian foodstores sell both fresh and dry lemongrass, sometimes under the Indonesian name *sereh*. Its rich lemon flavor and fragrance make it a tangy addition to many foods. Lemongrass can be taken medicinally as a digestive aid, and to relieve feverish complaints.

Description and parts used

Lemongrass is a tender perennial tropical grass, and can grow to nearly 6 ft. It is densely tufted with long, thin, fibrous leaves that, when crushed, are extremely fragrant, hence its name. The flowers are greenish with a red tinge, and appear in clusters in the summer. The bulbous base of the grass stems is the most widely used part in the kitchen. Lemongrass can be dried, and is available either in pieces or powdered.

❦ CULINARY USES ❦

The tender stalks of lemongrass can be chopped fine, and the leaves, once peeled, can be used in the same way as scallions to flavor casseroles, curries, and soups (see recipe opposite). The base of the leaves is used in a curry-like powder that is commonly used in southeast Asian cooking, especially with fish, chicken, and pork. Lemongrass combines particularly well with chilies, garlic, and shallots.

You can make an infusion of the dried leaves to be drunk as a relaxing herbal tea. The chopped fine fresh leaves can be floated on summer drinks, or use whole stalks as stirrers for a hint of citrus. You can also use lemongrass to flavor sugar syrups for fruit desserts. For specific preparation techniques, see page 87.

HOT AND SOUR SOUP

Try eating this soup when you are feeling slightly under the weather
or have the beginnings of a cold. The chilis in the soup help
clear the head and make you feel better. Serves 6.

INGREDIENTS

1/4 cup dried mushrooms
1 small chicken breast, skinned
6 oz tofu (bean curd), drained
3 cups chicken broth, preferably homemade
1 to 2 bird's eye chilies, deseeded and chopped
3 lemongrass stalks, bruised, outer leaves
   discarded
1 carrot, peeled and cut into thin strips
2 celery stalks, trimmed and cut into thin strips
3 tbsp dark soy sauce
1/4 cup snow peas, halved
1/2 cup bean sprouts
4 tbsp cornstarch
2 tbsp dry sherry
2 tbsp chopped fresh cilantro

METHOD

1 Soak the mushrooms in 2/3 cup very hot
   water for 20 minutes. Drain, setting aside
   the mushrooms and the liquid. Chop the
   rehydrated mushrooms into small pieces,
   if necessary.

2 Cut the chicken into thin strips and the tofu
   into small dice, and set them aside. Heat a
   wok, then add the broth with the chilies and
   lemongrass, and simmer for 3 minutes.

3 Add the mushrooms, liquid, chicken strips,
   tofu, carrot, celery, and soy sauce. Bring to
   a boil, and simmer for 2 minutes. Skim if
   necessary and add the snow peas and bean
   sprouts. Cook for another minute.

4 Blend the cornstarch with the sherry, stir
   into the wok, and cook, stirring until slightly
   thickened. Stir in the cilantro, heat for 30
   seconds, and serve.

CARDAMOM
Elettaria cardamomum

Related to ginger, cardamom is one of the oldest and most highly valued spices in the world. It is the most expensive spice after saffron and vanilla.

Today the most widely used variety of cardamon is grown in southern India. The Normans took cardamom to Britain from France in the eleventh century, where it was still popular in Tudor times. The cardamom spice consists of a pod of green inedible casing containing hard, brownish-black seeds. The spice has a mellow, enticing smell, with a strong lemon/camphor flavor. Cardamom taken medicinally is used to settle upset stomachs and to relieve respiratory disorders.

Description and parts used

The best cardamom comes from the rainforests of Malabar, where it grows as a shrub about 6 ft. tall, with yellow-tipped blue-streaked flowers that produce small fruit pods. They are picked and dried. The best pods are hard and greenish. Cardamom grows wild throughout India in the tropical mountain forests, and is cultivated in Sri Lanka, Thailand, and Central America.

❦ CULINARY USES ❦

You can either split the pods and use whole (remember to discard before serving), or remove the seeds from the casing and grind up before adding to a dish. Cardamom is used in curries and to flavor pilau rice. In the Arab world it is added to coffee and strong sweet tea as a sign of hospitality and generosity. In northern Europe it is used to flavor breads, pastries, and cakes (see opposite), and is used as a pickling spice.

Cardamom gives a delicious flavor when added to vanilla pie-fillings, ice cream, rice desserts, and stewed fruit. It is better to buy the whole pods and grind them yourself rather than buy cardamon ready ground (it loses its flavor so quickly when ground that it will already have deteriorated before it can be sold).

CARDAMOM AND ORANGE CUPCAKES

Cardamom's pungent aroma is delightful in Indian vegetable curries, drinks, and ice cream, and also in cakes and desserts. Makes 1½ dozen.

FOR THE CUPCAKES

½ lb (2 sticks) butter, softened
1 cup superfine sugar
2 cups self-rising flour
4 eggs
1 tsp ground cardamom
1 tsp orange extract

FOR THE FROSTING

2 cups confectioners' sugar, sifted
¼ lb (1 stick) sweet butter, softened
¼ cup sour cream
1½ tbsp shredded orange zest
1 tsp orange extract
36 cardamom pods (for decoration only)

METHOD

1 Preheat the oven to 350°F. Place 18 paper baking cups in muffin pans. Combine all the cupcake ingredients in a medium bowl and beat with an electric mixer until smooth and pale, about 2 to 3 minutes.

2 Spoon the batter into the cups. Bake in the oven for 20 minutes. Remove pans from the oven and cool for 5 minutes. Then remove the cupcakes and cool on a rack.

3 To make the frosting, beat the confectioners' sugar, butter, sour cream, orange zest, and orange extract with an electric mixer until smooth. Spread the frosting on the cupcakes and top each with 2 cardamom pods. Store unfrosted for up to 2 days in an airtight container, or freeze for up to 3 months.

CLOVES
Eugenia caryophyllus

*Strong and aromatic, cloves play a big part in herbal remedies and cooking.
The name comes from the Latin word* clavus, *meaning "nail," which
describes the clove's shape.*

Cloves are the dried flower buds of a tree, related to myrtle, and became known to Europeans by the fourth century. There is evidence that cloves were used in early Chinese herbal medicine, and the Romans and Greeks also used them.

Cloves can be used to scent a room—traditionally they are stuck into an orange and hung up as a scented pomander. An old remedy for toothache is to clamp a clove between the teeth or to rub clove oil on the tooth.

Description and parts used

The clove tree originally came from the Molucca Islands, but they are now cultivated in many parts of the world including the West Indies, Zanzibar, and Madagascar. The tree is an evergreen with bright red flowers. It grows very tall, even exceeding 50 ft. The flower buds turn reddish-brown when dried, and can then be used whole or ground.

🌿 CULINARY USES 🌿

If you use cloves whole, remember to remove them before serving, otherwise grind them and add directly to a dish. Cloves are one of the spices used in the Indian spice mix, garam masala (see page 153).

Cloves are versatile and can be used to flavor curries, broths, sauces, relishes, mulled wine, punches, apple dishes, dried fruit compotes, cakes, breads, mincemeat, and dried fruit desserts, as well as marinades and cooking sauces for meat and poultry dishes.

Note that you need very few of them—just half a dozen whole cloves in an apple pie will be sufficient to flavor it. Cloves are extremely aromatic, and should be kept tightly sealed in lidded glass jars to prevent scenting other ingredients.

PUMPKIN MUFFINS

The combined scents of ginger, nutmeg, and cloves will spice up your pumpkin for this fall treat. Makes 1 dozen.

INGREDIENTS
2²/₃ cups all-purpose flour
¹/₃ cup light brown sugar, packed
1 tbsp baking powder
¹/₂ tsp ground nutmeg
¹/₂ tsp ground cloves
1 tsp ground ginger
Pinch of salt
1 egg, lightly beaten
¹/₂ cup puréed pumpkin, fresh or canned
³/₄ cup fat-free milk
¹/₃ cup sunflower oil
3 tbsp chopped, candied ginger
4 tbsp pumpkin seeds

METHOD
1 Preheat the oven to 350°F. Grease a 12-cup muffin pan. In a bowl, combine the dry ingredients with a spoon.
2 In a large bowl, beat the egg, pumpkin, milk, and oil with an electric mixer until combined. Add the flour mixture to the pumpkin mixture, mixing until nearly combined.
3 Fold in the candied ginger, but do not overmix. Spoon the batter into the prepared pan. Sprinkle each muffin with a few pumpkin seeds. Bake for 20 minutes. Remove pan from the oven and cool for 5 minutes. Then remove the muffins and cool on a rack. Store in an airtight container for up to 2 days, or freeze for up to 3 months.

WASABI
Eutrema wasabia/Wasabia japonica

A spice from the creeping root of a Japanese plant whose name means "mountain hollyhock." It has a strong, pungent aroma and a strong, acrid, cleansing flavor.

Wasabi belongs to the same family as horseradish, radishes, and mustard, all of which contain pungent sulfur glycosides. The fresh root is seldom available fresh outside Japan, but wasabi powder or paste is available. Wasabi is also used as a digestive stimulant.

Description and parts used
Wasabi plants grow wild on the banks of mountain streams, and are cultivated in flooded mountain terraces. The stalks reach 16 in. in height, and the leaves are kidney-shaped. White flowers appear in summer. The brownish-green skin of the plant's root is removed, and then the pale green flesh is shredded and either used fresh, or dried and ground.

❧ CULINARY USES ❧

Powdered wasabi should be mixed with an equal amount of tepid water and left for 10 minutes for its flavor to develop. The ready-made paste loses its flavor more quickly than the powder. In Japan, wasabi is one of the most important culinary flavors. Wasabi is used as a condiment to go with raw fish (sashimi) and rice sushi with pickled ginger and dark soy sauce.

ASAFETIDA
Ferula assafoetida

Asafetida is an Asiatic spice little known outside India, where it is used in minute quantities to impart a delicious onion flavor.

The name derives from the Persian word *aza*, meaning "resin," and the Latin word *fetida*, meaning "stinking." Asafetida is a perennial plant that grows wild in Afghanistan and eastern Iran.

Description and parts used
Probably the most foul-smelling of all plants, this tall plant with its thick roots emits its distinct odor from all its parts. The thick stems are cut to the root, and the milky sap that flows out is collected as a resin. When the resin hardens it can be ground to a yellow to dark amber powder. This has an unpleasant, sulfurous odor, which disappears on cooking, leaving a milder, more pleasant onion flavoring.

❧ CULINARY USES ❧

In western and southern India, asafetida is mainly used in vegetarian curries and pulse dishes, but it can also be used to enhance the flavor of fish, meat, casseroles, sauces, and relishes. If it is not stored properly, its strong smell will contaminate other ingredients, so it should be kept quite separate from other spices in airtight, screw-topped glass jars.

FENNEL
Foeniculum vulgare

Fennel seeds have a warm, aromatic smell, with a fragrant, anise seed-like taste, and perk up a wide range of recipes for drinks, chicken dishes, and cakes.

LIQUORICE
Glycyrrhiza glabra

Licorice grows widely in the Mediterranean and all the way to China. It has a sweet, distinctive flavor and is widely used in confectionery and medicines.

The seeds of the pretty fennel plant make an interesting, tasty spice. Because fennel grows wild in so many temperate places, it is difficult to say where it originated, though many think it was in the Mediterranean. It was well known and much used by the ancient Chinese, Romans, Greeks, Britons, Indians, Egyptians, and Persians.

Description and parts used
Fennel has yellow flowery seed heads that are harvested just before the seeds ripen. The heads are dried and then the seeds are removed. They are greenish-yellow to brown, elongated, and oval with prominent ridges. They can be used whole or ground.

Its name means "sweet root," and it is cultivated for its flavor and medicinal properties throughout Europe, especially in Italy. It was once used as a cooking sweetener because it has 50 times the sweetening power of ordinary sugar. The root can be chewed or sucked to relieve sore throats and ease other cold symptoms. It also has gentle laxative properties, and is a popular agent in cough syrups used to disguise other less pleasant tasting ingredients.

Description and parts used
The individual flavor of licorice comes from the rhizome, which is harvested, boiled, and filtered, and from which the juice is extracted. As it cools, it solidifies into a black, sticky cake.

❦ CULINARY USES ❦

Fennel is extremely versatile. The seeds, dried and crushed, can be used to make a refreshing tea or can be added to fish and chicken dishes. They are often sprinkled on the top of bread and cakes, or are added to fruit salads and compotes. The leaves can be used as an herb (see page 40), and the stalks can be cooked as a vegetable accompaniment, or eaten raw in a salad.

❦ CULINARY USES ❦

Licorice can be used to add a very strong flavor to beers and liqueurs. You can buy commercially produced licorice in its sticky black cake form or as a dried rhizome. It helps reduce the acidity of rhubarb. **Caution: Under some circumstances licorice can lead to a rise in blood pressure, and is best avoided if you have high blood pressure. Avoid during pregnancy.**

STAR ANISE
Illicium verum

*One of the most instantly recognizable spices, it's easy to see
how star anise gets its name: the fruit is shape like an
eight-pointed star, and tastes like anise seed.*

Although unrelated to anise seed, you will find the spicy, sweet taste of star anise is similar but stronger. Its essential oil is virtually the same, so both plants have the same aroma. In China, it is used as a food seasoning and in herbal medicine. In the West, it is often added to fish casseroles. Its essential oil, which is known as oil of anise seed, is used to flavor liqueurs, such as pastis in Italy, Germany, and France. The seeds of star anise can be chewed to sweeten the breath. Star anise is a natural diuretic and appetite stimulant.

Description and parts used

Star anise is the fruit of an evergreen tree related to magnolia, which originated in the East Indies but is now cultivated widely in China. The fruits have eight brown seeds and are first harvested when the tree is six years old. It continues to be fruitful for many years. The fruits are dried and can be used whole or ground.

❦ CULINARY USES ❦

The Chinese use star anise in many dishes, especially duck, chicken, and pork recipes (see opposite) and the ground seeds are often added to coffee and tea to enhance their flavor. The oil is used to flavor drinks. If you need a strong anise seed flavor in cooking, it is even better to use star anise than anise seed. Its beautiful shape makes it an attractive addition to fruit salads, syrups, and compotes—although inedible it is worth leaving in a recipe and using as a decoration. Keep the seeds in a screw-topped glass jar to preserve their flavor.

Caution: Do not confuse this spice with Japanese star anise (*Illicium religiosum*), which is poisonous. You can tell the difference by the smell: Japanese star anise smells like denatured alcohol.

CHINESE RED ROAST PORK

A sumptuous Chinese meal enriched by rice wine and sherry vinegar
featuring soft, succulent pork that melts in the mouth. Serves 4.

INGREDIENTS

1lb piece lean pork fillet

6 tbsp dark soy sauce

2 tbsp Chinese rice wine or sweet sherry

2 star anise, ground

2 garlic cloves, peeled and fine chopped

1in piece gingerroot, peeled and fine chopped

4 tbsp superfine sugar

2 tbsp rice or sherry vinegar

Fresh cilantro and red chilis to garnish

METHOD

1 Trim any fat and silver skin from the pork; place
pork in a shallow dish. Mix together the soy
sauce, rice wine, star anise, garlic, and ginger.

2 Spoon the spice mixture over the pork, cover,
and chill for at least 4 hours or overnight,
turning occasionally.

3 Preheat the oven to 350°F. Drain the pork,
reserving the marinade, and place on a
roasting rack over a roasting pan. Half fill
the pan with boiling water. Cook in the oven,
basting occasionally with the marinade, for
about an hour, until the pork is cooked.

4 Just before the end of cooking, put the sugar
in a small saucepan with the vinegar and heat
gently until the sugar dissolves. Bring to a
boil and simmer for 3 to 4 minutes until the
sugar mixture is syrupy.

5 When the pork is cooked, drain the water,
and keeping the pork on the rack, brush
generously with the sugar syrup. Allow
to stand for 10 minutes, then slice and
serve hot or allow to cool and serve cold
with egg fried rice and extra dark soy
sauce for dipping.

JUNIPER
Juniperus communis

*here are many different forms of juniper, from the common
juniper used in medicine and in cooking, to the
red cedars of North America.*

Some junipers contain an oil that is poisonous which is why juniper has long been considered a magic plant for warding off evil and evil spirits. It was often burned in rooms occupied by the sick to fumigate the air and to drive out demons. Today the berries of the tree are well known as the spice that flavors gin and other cordials; in fact, its Latin name comes from the Dutch word *genever* which means "gin." In medicine, juniper is used in the treatment of urinary tract infections and for gout and rheumatism. It can reduce inflammation of the digestive system.

Description and parts used

Juniper is widespread throughout the world. It grows as a small evergreen shrub or a tree reaching about 9 ft. tall. It carries cones, the females of which turn into berries. The berries start off green and slowly turn black and ripen over a three-year period.

❦ CULINARY USES ❦

Dried juniper berries are added to patés, game, and venison dishes (see recipe opposite) and to marinades. Traditionally they have been used with game because the berries work well to lessen the strong "gamey" taste, which some dislike. The berries blend well with garlic and the strong, woody-flavored herbs, such as rosemary and thyme.

Fresh berries are used to make a preserve to accompany cold meats. Juniper also goes well with the flavor of purple fruits, such as damsons, plums, blackberries, and blueberries. The leaves can be used fresh or dried with broiled fish, and the wood and leaves can be used on a barbecue to give a subtle flavor to meat. **Caution: Avoid juniper during pregnancy.**

VENISON WITH JUNIPER AND BLACKBERRIES

The strong taste of game is matched by a deep, subtle mix
of juniper berries, port, and redcurrant jelly. Serves 4.

INGREDIENTS

4 (5-oz) venison steaks, trimmed
Salt and freshly ground black pepper
1 tbsp juniper berries, crushed
2 tbsp butter
1 small red onion, peeled and fine chopped
8 oz blackberries, washed and hulled
2 tbsp ruby port
2 tbsp blackberry or raspberry vinegar
2 tbsp redcurrant jelly
2 tbsp fine chopped fresh parsley

METHOD

1 Wash and pat dry the venison with paper
towels. Season on both sides with salt, pepper,
and juniper, rubbing in the seasoning. Cover
and chill for 30 minutes.

2 Melt the butter in a skillet until bubbling and
cook the venison steaks for 3 to 4 minutes on
each side—this will cook them to medium—or
until cooked to your liking. Drain the venison
steaks, reserving the juices, and keep warm.

3 Gently fry the onion for 5 minutes in the
reserved juices until softened, but not
browned. Stir in the blackberries and port,
bring to a boil, cover and simmer for
5 minutes until softened.

4 Stir in the vinegar and redcurrant jelly and
heat gently until melted.

5 To serve, spoon the blackberries and sauce
over each medallion of venison and sprinkle
with chopped parsley.

6 Serve with sautéed potatoes and a selection
of broiled mushrooms.

AMCHOOR / MANGO POWDER
Mangifera indica

Mango fruit is also available in a dried, powdered form, and can be added to a range of Indian recipes, injecting a lively hint of sharpness.

Native to India, mango fruit is one of the most popular of all tropical fruits. Amchoor is made from the unripe fruit, which has a tart, rather than a sweet, flavor. The flesh is dried and ground to make a powder. It is used as a souring agent and can be bought from most good Indian grocery stores.

Description and parts used

Unripe windfall mangoes are gathered, sliced, and dried until they turn light brown.

The pieces are then ground to make a sand-colored lumpy powder, and although there is little smell there is a sharp, acidic flavor similar to tart citrus fruit.

❦ CULINARY USES ❦

Amchoor is most commonly used in northern Indian vegetarian cooking. It is added to vegetable curries and soups to give a sharp flavor, similar to tamarind. Amchoor is often combined with mint, ginger, ajowan, cayenne, grenadine seeds, and cumin seeds to make Chal Masala. In the Middle East it is used to tenderize meat and fish. It is also added to stuffings for breads.

CURRY LEAF
Murrya koenigii

This is one of those spices that really is best grown and bought in the East where it is available fresh. It gives extra spark to curries, adding a deeper flavor.

In India and Sri Lanka curry leaf is added to curries to increase the flavor, and it is grown throughout Asia for this purpose; the fresh leaves are widely available. Curry leaves come from a small, ornamental tree that grows wild in the Himalayan foothills. In the West only dried leaves are available, but they have little flavor and need to be used by the handful to obtain a good curry flavor.

Description and parts used

Curry leaf grows only in tropical regions, and is not really suited to temperate climates unless it is grown in a greenhouse. The leaves resemble small bay leaves and are used on the stalk.

❦ CULINARY USES ❦

Curry leaves should be added fresh to curries and spicy meat dishes, rice dishes, and soups. They are the essential ingredient in hot curry powder, providing its unique aroma and flavor. The leaves should be removed before serving. The dried leaves have almost no flavor, but the powdered leaves do and can sometimes be bought in stores specializing in Indian food. Good storage preserves its flavor.

MACE
Myristica fragrans

*Mace is the bright red, shiny fiber that covers the nutmeg seed
inside the fruit of the nutmeg tree. The flavor
is refined, rich, and warm.*

The nutmeg tree produces both mace and nutmeg. Mace is the weblike flesh, or aril, that covers the seed kernel of the fruit. Believed to have originated in the Molucca Islands of the East Indies, it is now cultivated in many countries such as Indonesia, Brazil, Sri Lanka, and the West Indies. Arab traders spread the use of mace throughout the Arab world and all over Europe. During Tudor times in England it was considered one of the finest spices available. Medicinally, it can be used to treat stomach disorders.

Description and parts used

When dried, mace becomes brittle and turns from red to brownish-yellow. Indonesian mace is usually orange-red, and mace from Grenada orange-yellow. It is available whole as "blades," or ground.

NUTMEG
Myristica fragrans

*The inner seed of the nutmeg tree, lying inside the filigree covering
(or aril) of mace, is the nutmeg that's widely used to
flavor everything from ice cream to cookies.*

Nutmegs are quite large, about ½ in. long, and extremely hard. For this reason they are never used whole but always grated. The flavor is sweeter than that of mace, and has a fresh, warming aftertaste. Once introduced to Europe in the sixteenth century, nutmeg became important as a spice and medicine. By the eighteenth century people carried nutmegs with them to use as a seasoning. Nutmeg is used in treating the digestive system.

Description and parts used

Nutmeg trees are found in hot, tropical places and are extremely difficult to grow. The nutmeg has always been cheaper to produce than mace because it requires little processing before it is sold, whereas mace has to be dried carefully to prevent decay. Once the ovular, gray-brown seed is separated from the nutmeg, it is allowed to dry. The oil of small or damaged nutmeg seeds is extracted and used in the cosmetic industry. Nutmegs are sold whole or ground.

❦ CULINARY USES ❦

Nutmeg can be grated in small quantities into hot, spicy drinks, such as mulled wine or even hot chocolate, and used to flavor and sweeten desserts. You can grate nutmeg over baked dishes (see recipe opposite), vanilla pie-fillings, and ice cream. It is a tasty addition to stewed fruit. In the Dutch kitchen, nutmeg is widely used in vegetable purées and mashed potato, and the Italians use the spice to season meat for pasta sauces. Nutmeg is its own best storage container, and whole spices will keep three or four years. Small quantities can be shredded from the whole nutmeg when needed.

Caution: Nutmeg contains myristicin, a hallucinatory compound, which can be poisonous in certain amounts. As little as two whole nutmegs could be enough to cause death.

BAKED LASAGNE

This dish tastes best with the concentrated flavor of dried porcini. Nutmeg adds depth to any sauce that features cream or cheese. Serves 4 to 6.

INGREDIENTS

3 oz dried porcini

2 cups water

8 shallots, chopped

5 tbsp butter

3 tbsp brandy

1½ cups light cream

Salt, ground black pepper, and a few gratings of nutmeg, to taste

10 oz precooked lasagne sheets

6 oz freshly shredded Parmesan cheese

5 tbsp fresh chervil leaves, roughly chopped

METHOD

1 Preheat an oven to 375°F. Place the porcini and water in a saucepan and bring to a boil. Reduce the heat and simmer over medium heat for 5 to 10 minutes, or until the mushrooms have softened.

2 Remove the mushrooms from the liquid, chop roughly, and set aside. Strain the liquid for the sauce.

3 Sauté the shallots in the butter until softened, then add the mushrooms and cook for a few moments. Add the brandy, and cook over high heat until evaporated. Ladle in ½ cup of the mushroom liquid, and cook over high heat until nearly evaporated.

4 Repeat until all the liquid is used up and you have a concentrated, thin reduction. Now add the cream and simmer for 5 to 10 minutes. Season with salt, pepper, and nutmeg, and set aside.

5 In a 12 x 15 inch buttered baking pan, place a layer of lasagne sheets. Ladle in about a quarter of the mushroom sauce, a quarter of the cheese, and a sprinkling of the chervil. Repeat the layers until mixture is used up, ending with the cheese and reserving the final sprinkling of chervil until serving.

6 Bake in the oven for 25 to 30 minutes, or until the cheese is melted and lightly browned in places. Serve immediately, with the reserved chervil scattered over.

NIGELLA
Nigella sativa

*Grown across a huge area from India to Egypt, the peppery nigella
seeds can be used to flavor curries, meat dishes,
sauces, and cooked vegetables.*

Nigella is known by many other names
including nutmeg flower, black cumin,
Roman coriander, and fennel flower. It is a
popular spice in Turkey and Tunisia, as well
as in Greece, Egypt, and India. It grows wild
throughout the whole of Asia and the Middle
East, where it has traditionally been used as
we use black pepper.

It is related to *N. damascena* (love-in-a-
mist), with which it is often confused. The
two plants are very similar, but only *N. sativa*
should be used as a spice. The seeds of love-in-
a-mist are distilled for an essential oil used in
perfumes and lipsticks.

Description and parts used

The flowers of *N. sativa* are small and white
with a blue tinge. The seed capsules are
gathered as they ripen, before they burst open.
They are dried and crushed to remove the dull
black seeds that can be used whole or ground.

❧ CULINARY USES ❧

In India, where the seeds are called *kalonji*
or black onion seeds, they are used as a
pickling spice, often being added to mango
chutney. The flavor is nutty and acrid, with a
faint flavor of oregano.

The seeds are said to benefit digestion and
they are usually dry roasted before using to
increase their aroma and flavor. The seeds
are also commonly added to vegetable
curries, pulse dishes, and sprinkled over
cooked rice pilaus. The Bengalis use them
mainly as a flavoring for fish dishes.

The seeds can also be ground in a pepper
mill and then used in the same way as
black pepper. They can even be added to
breads and pastries to give a little extra
bite and pungency.

POPPY
Papaver somniferum

Poppy seeds are an invaluable extra, proving a nutty topping for various pastries and cakes, though they can even be tossed on classic Italian dishes such as pasta.

The tiny blue-black seeds of the lilac-colored opium poppy, as it is commonly called, were used as a spice by the Sumerians around 4,000 BC. Opium poppies grow wild in the Middle East, and were first taken to China 1,000 years ago. They have been used for their pain-relieving properties in ancient Greece, Egypt, Italy, India, and the Middle East. Today they are cultivated for use as a culinary spice with a nutty flavor, and for their medicinal qualities, being used to make morphine and codeine.

Description and parts used

The red poppy plant grows around 4 ft. tall, though there is also a variety with white flowers. When the seed heads turn yellow-brown, the plants are usually harvested mechanically. The heads are cut off and dried, and the tiny hard seeds removed. Indian seeds are cream-yellow in color, brown in Turkey, and slate-gray in Europe.

❦ CULINARY USES ❦

Cakes of poppy seeds and honey were given to the athletes of ancient Greece to increase vigor. The seeds are best dry roasted to bring out their flavor. In Middle Eastern cooking, the seeds are used to flavor sweet dishes and to make cakes, desserts, and strudel fillings. In India, the seeds are called *khas khas* and are used to flavor meat dishes. In most European countries, the seeds are sprinkled onto newly baked bread. Try tossing seeds into cooked pasta or noodles to add texture and nuttiness.

Caution: In some countries there may be a legal restriction on growing opium poppies because all parts of the plant, except the seeds, are poisonous. The seeds should not be taken by those suffering from hay fever or any allergic condition.

ALLSPICE
Pimento officinalis

*Allspice is a three-in-one spice, which tastes of cinnamon, nutmeg, and cloves.
As a medicine, it is said to improve digestion and
aid the nervous system.*

Allspice is also known as Jamaican pepper and pimento, though all these names are inaccurate because it's neither a spice combination nor a pepper. It is said to have been taken to Europe from Jamaica by Christopher Columbus, while the Aztecs used it to flavor chocolate.

The name "allspice" was invented by John Ray, a seventeenth-century English botanist, who identified its three flavors.

Description and parts used

Allspice is the dried fruit of a tree that is native to Central and South America. The tree can grow to an enormous height—over 50 ft.—and is cultivated in Jamaica on plantations known as pimento walks.

The flowers are small and white, and the fruits are gathered unripe and dried in the hot sun until they turn reddish-brown. It can be bought whole or ground.

❦ CULINARY USES ❦

Allspice is best bought whole so that it can be freshly ground as needed. You can use it in much the same way you would use either cinnamon, nutmeg, or cloves in hot, spicy drinks and mulled wine, as a pickling spice, and for desserts, and vanilla pie-fillings. Just a small amount adds zing to baked goods (see recipe opposite).

Allspice can also be used for meat and fish dishes to impart an unusual, spicy flavor. It is especially good with lamb, and some say it tastes of juniper berries (see page 128). You can add it as a powder to curry dishes and use it to flavor shellfish. Try adding a couple of berries to your pepper mill to add a little zest to your black pepper. The leaves are used to make bay rum, and the flowers can be infused for a tea.

CARROT CUPCAKES

These delicious cupcakes are perfect for those monitoring the sugar levels in their diet. Makes 1 dozen.

INGREDIENTS

$^{1}/_{2}$ cup light vegetable oil

$^{1}/_{2}$ cup brown sugar, packed

1 egg, lightly beaten

3 egg whites

1 cup shredded carrots

1 cup shredded cooking apples

1 cup (7 oz) raisins

$^{1}/_{2}$ cup ($3^{1}/_{2}$ oz) chopped dates

$^{1}/_{2}$ cup ($3^{1}/_{2}$ oz) mixed dried berries

$^{1}/_{2}$ cup ($3^{1}/_{2}$ oz) chopped walnuts

1 tsp ground allspice

1 tsp baking powder

$2^{3}/_{4}$ cups self-rising whole wheat flour

METHOD

1 Preheat the oven to 350°F. Place 12 paper baking cups into a muffin pan. In a large bowl, combine the oil and sugar, and beat with an electric mixer until light and smooth, about 2 to 3 minutes.

2 Beat the egg and egg whites, one at a time, and then add the carrots, apples, dried fruits, and walnuts. Sift the rest of the ingredients into a medium mixing bowl. Add them to the carrot mixture, stirring until just combined.

3 Spoon the mixture into the cups. Bake for 20 minutes. Remove pan from the oven and cool for 5 minutes. Then remove the cupcakes and cool on a rack. Serve with butter. Store in an airtight container for up to 3 days, or freeze for up to 3 months.

ANISE SEED (ANISE)
Pimpinella anisum

*The oval-shaped, aromatic seeds are one of the world's oldest
known spices and are probably best known for
flavoring the popular Greek drink, ouzo.*

Smelling and tasting slightly sweet with a distinct hint of licorice, anise seed was first cultivated by the ancient Egyptians and then spread throughout the Arab, Roman, and Greek worlds. The Romans were the first to really use this piquant spice to flavor their cakes, which they ate after heavy meals to settle their stomachs. Anise seed grows wild throughout the Middle East, but it can also be cultivated in any moderately warm climate. The oil is used in the production of toothpaste, and anise-seed tea is used to settle and improve digestion; it also has warming properties good for stimulating the circulation.

Description and parts used

The plant grows to about 1¹/₂ ft. high. It has broad leaves and small, cream-colored flowers that give way to tiny, oval, light brown, hairy seeds. The seeds often have the stalk attached, and are available whole or ground.

🌿 CULINARY USES 🌿

In Europe, anise seed is used as a cake and cookie spice, and in the Middle East and India it is added to soups, casseroles, and breads. Use anise seeds whole, or crush lightly. The seeds can also be chewed to aid digestion and sweeten the breath after a meal. Anise seed is a traditional flavoring for sweets and confectionery; because it is mild to the taste, it is a popular choice with both children and adults.

The oil is extracted and used to flavor various liqueurs, such as Pernod, pastis, and arak. The fresh leaves have a delicate flavor, and can be used to flavor curries and spicy meat dishes. Like most spices, it is best to grind your own anise seed as it quickly loses its aroma and flavor when ground. Do not confuse with star anise (see page 126).

CUBEB (JAVA PEPPER)
Piper cubeba

Cubeb is an unusual and very hot spice grown in Sumatra, Penang, and New Guinea. It's the unripe fruit of a climbing plant that grows like a vine, and is related to black pepper—but it's got much more clout!

Dried, unripe cubeb berries look the same as the dried berries of black pepper—although cubeb is a lot more fiery and aromatic. Because of its warming properties, cubeb is said to relieve bronchial and sinus infections.

Description and parts used

Cubeb grows well in subtropical forests. The fruits are picked unripe before being dried; the peppercornlike berries have little tails attached and have a wrinkled, leathery appearance, and are bought whole or ground. Cubeb is distilled for its oil, which is used commercially to flavor sauces, relishes, and bitters, and in the perfume industry.

🐾 CULINARY USES 🐾

Use sparingly because it's quite strong and bitter. The spice is used in Indonesian food as a hot, spicy addition to rice dishes, curries, and fish. It can be used to replace allspice when necessary, or as a general seasoning in the same way as black pepper.

LONG PEPPER
Piper longum

Barely heard of in Europe and North America, long pepper is common in Asia where it is rated for its flavor, which is like a sweeter form of black pepper.

The plant is related to black pepper, and is known in Sanskrit as *pippali* from which the name "pepper" originates.

Long pepper spread throughout southern Asia before black pepper, and was probably the first type of pepper to arrive in the Mediterranean, where the Romans prized its combination of hot, spicy, and sweet.

Description and parts used

The main difference between black peppercorns and long pepper is the shape. Long pepper consists of many small fruits about the size of poppy seeds. They grow together to form spikes about 1 in. long that are gray-black and resemble elongated pine cones.

🐾 CULINARY USES 🐾

Long pepper is seldom found outside Eastern Asia, where it is always used whole as a cooking spice and to flavor pickles and preserves. If crushed with a pestle and mortar it can be sprinkled onto broiled steak or barbecued meat.

PEPPER
Piper nigrum

Peppercorns don't have to be black. They are available in several colors, and all have a slightly different flavor, making them indispensable in the kitchen.

Originally a native of the Malabar Coast, pepper now grows in tropical regions all over the world. The white, green, and pink peppercorns all come from the same plant. Black pepper has a strong, pungent flavor; white pepper has a milder flavor but is less aromatic; and pink pepper is more aromatic than pungent.

Description and parts used

The pepper vine produces flowers that fall to reveal clusters of green berries. The berries are picked unripe and green and are allowed to dry in the sun. Berries that ripen on the vine turn red, and they are sold as pink pepper, pickled in brine or freeze-dried. If the ripe berries are picked and soaked to get rid of the outer red husk, the inner, skinless peppercorn can be dried and sold as white pepper. Green unripe berries can be bought fresh in clusters, or pickled in brine, or they are freeze-dried.

❧ CULINARY USES ❧

There are few dishes that do not benefit from a little black pepper at the end of cooking. White pepper is generally used in pale-colored dishes in which the use of black pepper would spoil the appearance—and it has a slightly sweeter flavor. Whole peppercorns are a better buy than the ready-ground kind that lose their flavor very quickly. Lightly crushed peppercorns can be rubbed into meat before cooking (see recipe opposite) and they are often used whole in pickles and marinades.

Surprisingly, perhaps, the strong taste of pepper also goes well with very sweet strawberries, adding an interesting tang if served as an appetizer. Pepper contains an oil that helps stimulate the digestion of meat and high-protein foods.

STEAK AU POIVRE

You've never had a steak like this before—bursting with peppercorns,
brandy, mustard, and cream. Serves 2.

INGREDIENTS

2 (5-oz) fillet steaks
1 tbsp cracked pepper, crushed
2 tbsp olive oil
2 tbsp butter
1 garlic clove, peeled and fine chopped
1 tsp Dijon mustard
3 tbsp brandy
2 tsp green peppercorns in brine, drained
Scant ¹/₂ cup light cream
Salt

METHOD

1 Cover the steaks with plastic wrap and
   tenderize with a rolling pin until flattened to
   a thickness of ¹/₂ in. Set aside.

2 On a small plate, mix the crushed pepper with
   the olive oil, and coat both sides of each steak
   in the mixture.

3 Heat a skillet over a high heat for 30 seconds,
   add the steaks and cook for 3 to 4 minutes
   on each side or until cooked to your liking.
   Remove from the skillet, reserving the juices,
   and keep warm.

4 In the same skillet, melt the butter and
   gently fry the garlic for about 2 minutes until
   softened but not browned. Add the mustard
   and brandy.

5 Bring to a boil and simmer for 2 minutes. Add
   the green peppercorns and cream, and heat
   through without boiling.

6 Season with salt, pour the sauce over the
   steaks and serve.

SUMAC
Rhus coriaria

*It might not be that well known in the West, but sumac
is worth tracking down to give recipes an
extra flash of tangy seasoning.*

Related to poison ivy, there are over 250 varieties of sumac, and some are quite poisonous. There are two distinct types that can be used as spices: the Middle Eastern *R. coriaria*, known as Sicilian sumac, and the North American *R. aromatica*. Sumac is not very well known in the West but can be procured from some Middle Eastern stores in its ground form, which is deep rusty red. Sumac is valued for its high tannin content and its astringent flavor, and the Romans used sumac as a souring agent before lemons were available in Europe.

Description and parts used

The sumac shrub grows tall and wild on the mountains of the Middle East. The leaves turn rusty red in the fall, and it bears spikes of tart red berries. The fruits are collected when ripe, allowed to dry and then powdered for culinary use. The bark is stripped off and used with the leaves as a dye.

❦ CULINARY USES ❦

The seeds are crushed and then steeped in water to extract the juice. You can also buy sumac powder, which you add to savory dishes to give a sharpish bite. It gives a fruity, sour flavor to a dish, in the same way as lemon or vinegar.

In the Middle East, sumac is taken as a sour drink to relieve mild stomach complaints. In the Lebanon and Syria, it is sprinkled over fish. In Turkey, powdered sumac is commonly added to hummus and salads, both to enhance the flavor and to act as a decoration. It makes a tangy seasoning for chicken or for lamb kebabs.

Add to a stuffing for meat, or try mixing with the yogurt, onion, and cucumber dip, tzaziki, for added flavor.

SESAME
Sesamum indicum

*Sesame is a native of India, Indonesia, Africa, and China,
and is a valuable and important addition
to any cook's spice cupboard.*

Sesame is one of the earliest spices known to have been used both for its seeds and oil. It was used in Egypt around 5,000 years ago, and there is evidence that it was being cultivated commercially in India as far back as 1,600BC. Sesame was even once believed to have had magical powers. Ali Baba's famous phrase "open sesame" probably springs from the pods' tendency to burst open suddenly. The seeds have a sweet, nutty flavor when lightly dry roasted.

Description and parts used

Sesame grows well in sandy soil and a hot climate. It is a tall annual with white, trumpet-shaped flowers that turn into seed capsules about 1 in. long. The small, flat seeds are beige or black depending on variety. Varieties have been developed to stop the pods bursting open and make them easier to harvest. Sesame seed oil is extracted and bottled as a flavoring.

❦ CULINARY USES ❦

The ground sesame seed is used to make the strong-tasting paste, tahini, which is a major ingredient used to make hummus (see page 105). In Greek cuisine the paste is made into halva, a sweetmeat commonly eaten with strong coffee.

Sesame seeds are also sprinkled onto bread, cakes, and pastries to give a nutty topping, or they can be mixed into caramelized sugar and left to set in slabs to make a nutty, brittle candy.

Toasted sesame seeds can be added to vegetables and cheese sauces and be used instead of breadcrumbs on fish pies, or sprinkled on soups and salads to give texture. Black seeds and sesame oil are used widely in Chinese cooking as a flavoring.

TAMARIND
Tamarindus indica

If you like lemons and limes, try tamarind. Slightly sharp, it gives extra edge to a wide range of meals and refreshing drinks.

The fruit of the tamarind tree is a dark brown bean, also called an Indian date, which has been cultivated for centuries. It is widely used in Indian cooking and also in that of southeast Asia, Africa, Iraq, and the countries bordering the Persian Gulf.

In sixteenth-century England, it was appreciated in a thirst-quenching drink, but today it is popular as a snack. The taste can be described as sweet, sour, aromatic, and fruity.

Description and parts used

The tamarind tree grows to a height of some 100 ft. and can reach more than 30 ft. wide. It is now cultivated in the West Indies. The fruits can be eaten fresh or dried, and the pulp is used to make a souring agent.

❦ CULINARY USES ❦

Tamarind can be purchased as a fibrous, black, sticky pulp known as tamarind paste, which is the husk without the seeds. You extract the flavor by soaking the paste in lightly sugared hot water, before squeezing it. It is a useful flavor to add to curries, meat, or fish, and has a souring action greater than either lemon or lime juice. It is also available in a dried and ground form.

AJOWAN
Trachyspermum ammi

If you like Indian or Asian food, ajowan is a "must" for anything from pickles and relishes to snacks and pastries.

Cultivated primarily for its essential oil, ajowan is a native of southern India, and is related to caraway and cumin. Indian recipes sometimes refer to it as lovage, ajwain, or carom, and it is a popular culinary seasoning spice throughout the country. It contains the same oil as the herb thyme, and on cooking has a slightly similar flavor. The seeds are also taken to relieve indigestion.

Description and parts used

The ajowan plant grows up to 2 ft. high and resembles wild parsley. It is also grown in Afghanistan, Pakistan, Iran, and Egypt. The seeds are small, oval, brownish-red, and resemble celery seeds. Once the seeds ripen, they are threshed and dried.

❦ CULINARY USES ❦

The seeds are easily crushed between thumb and forefinger. Once crushed, they become very aromatic. They can be used in many dishes as a substitute for thyme (see page 72) or lovage (see page 49), but note their taste is stronger. In India, ajowan is used to flavor paratha bread, crispy snacks, and pastries. Also good as a flavoring for pickles, relishes, and preserves.

FENUGREEK
Trigonella foenum-graecum

Fenugreek is grown throughout the world for its medicinal and culinary uses. The seeds have a mild curry flavor and a bitter aftertaste. It is probably best known in the West for its use in the Middle Eastern sweetmeat, halva.

Fenugreek is grown because it can add nitrogen to the soil, and it's often used today in the East as cattle fodder. It is also a good source of protein.

Fenugreek was probably first grown and recognized as a useful spice in Assyria around the seventh century BC. It spread to India and China, and is now used worldwide. In Egypt, it is sold as a dried plant called *hilba*, and was once used in embalming lotions. The seeds can be infused and used to treat gastric inflammation and digestive disorders.

Description and parts used

When the seeds are ripe, the plants are pulled up and dried. The seeds are threshed and dried again, and are either used whole or powdered. Fenugreek seeds are yellow-brown, hard and resemble tiny pebbles. The leaves are picked in summer and are either used fresh as an herb, or dried to make infusions.

🍃 CULINARY USES 🍃

The seeds can be lightly roasted to reduce the bitter aftertaste, and are an ingredient in curry powder (see page 153). The seeds can be allowed to sprout like mustard and cress, and are used as a delicious salad ingredient. The ground seeds are used in pickles, relishes, and chutneys. In Ethiopia, Yemen, and Libya it is ground to a paste and served as a condiment, or is added to bread and vegetable dishes. You can use the seeds in fried foods, casseroles, and pastries. The protein content makes it a useful spice for a vegetarian or vegan diet.

Caution: The seeds should not be taken by pregnant women because they contain saponin, an active agent that is used in oral contraceptives, and that can induce a miscarriage.

VANILLA
Vanilla planifolia

Real vanilla is very expensive and though cheaper imitations have been developed, they are far inferior in flavor. True vanilla has a rich, mellow, sweet aroma with a flavor to match.

Vanilla is the bean of a climbing orchid from South America, where the Aztecs used it to flavor chocolate. The Spanish took vanilla back to Europe and gave it its name (from *vaina* meaning pod or bean), and it has become one of the world's most important flavorings.

Description and parts used

The vanilla vine bears waxy greenish flowers that are fertilized by hummingbirds. In countries where there are no hummingbirds, the flowers have to be pollinated by hand, for example, in Indonesia, which now produces around 80 percent of the world's supply. The long, thin beans are picked green and unripe. During the lengthy drying process they turn a rich, dark brown, and the best develop white crystals of *vanillin* on the outside that provide its flavor. Vanilla essence is made from crushed beans soaked in alcohol, but it is very concentrated so use sparingly.

❧ CULINARY USES ❧

Use the whole bean to infuse creams with the vanilla flavor from the crystals. Use either whole or split down the middle to reveal the sticky dark paste and tiny black seeds. Vanilla is used to flavor vanilla pie-fillings, ice creams, cakes, cookies, rice desserts, mousses, and soufflés, and creamy drinks, such as iced coffee (see recipe opposite) or hot chocolate. Also try adding to a light cream sauce to go with scallops or large shrimp.

If you use whole beans, they can be carefully dried, stored, and then reused. Keep them submerged in white sugar in an airtight container. The beans will flavor the sugar as well. If you want a clean vanilla finish with no visible seeds, try using a good-quality extract as an alternative.

ICED VANILLA COFFEE

A delicious creamy treat—the ideal way to enjoy coffee when the
weather is warm. Serves 4.

INGREDIENTS
2¼ cups freshly brewed, hot, strong coffee
4 tbsp light brown sugar, packed
2 vanilla beans, split
Whipped cream (optional)
Ground nutmeg (optional)

METHOD
1 Pour the hot coffee into a heatproof pitcher
  and stir in the sugar until it dissolves.
2 Add the vanilla beans. Cover and chill for at
  least 2 hours.
3 Strain the coffee into tall glasses. Serve with
  whipped cream and a fine dusting of nutmeg.

SZECHUAN PEPPER
Zanthoxylum piperitum

*Szechuan pepper is a stimulant that works on the spleen
and stomach. It is very warming, and is good for
relieving the symptoms of colds and flu.*

Szechuan pepper has many other names, including anise pepper, fagara, Japanese pepper, Chinese pepper, and, rather charmingly, flower pepper, which comes from its Cantonese name *fahjiu*.

A warming stimulant, Szechuan pepper can be used as a condiment in the same way as pepper, but it is much hotter and more aromatic and woody, and should be used in smaller quantities. In ancient times it was used to flavor foods and wines that were offered to the gods.

Description and parts used

Szechuan pepper grows in the Szechuan region of China where, though a large tree, it's now mainly cultivated as a shrub. The leaves are picked fresh and used in cooking, and the bark is stripped and dried for infusions and decoctions or concentrates. The red-brown berries are picked in summer just before they fully ripen, and are dried to make the peppercorns.

❧ CULINARY USES ❧

The taste of Chinese cuisine was often considered somewhat subtle in Europe and North America—until the discovery of Szechuan cooking. With its fiery pepper sauces and hot curries, northern Chinese dishes quickly became some of the world's favorites, mainly thanks to the liberal use of Szechuan pepper.

The pepper is used to season shellfish (see recipe opposite), meat, and poultry, and especially Szechuan crispy duck. For increased flavor, dry roast the berries before grinding. The leaves can be used to flavor soups and meat dishes. They can be boiled with sugar and soy sauce, and even be covered in batter and fried. Szechuan pepper is an essential ingredient in five-spice powder (see page 152).

SZECHUAN-SAUTÉED SHRIMP

This crunchy, spicy plate of shrimp is enlivened by the Szechuan pepper
and gingerroot. Serves 4.

INGREDIENTS

16 large unpeeled raw shrimp, thawed if frozen
2 tbsp light soy sauce plus extra for dipping
1 tbsp Chinese rice wine or sweet sherry
$^1/_2$ tsp ground Szechuan pepper
1-in-piece gingerroot, peeled and chopped fine
2 scallions, trimmed and chopped fine
1 tbsp vegetable oil

METHOD

1 Wash and pat dry the shrimp and place in a
  shallow dish. Mix the soy sauce with the rice
  wine, pepper, gingerroot, and scallions and
  sprinkle over the shrimp. Cover and chill for at
  least 2 hours.

2 Heat the oil in a wok or large skillet. Drain the
  shrimp and stir fry for 3–4 minutes until pink
  all over. Drain and serve hot or cold on a bed
  of salad, with extra soy sauce for dipping.

GINGER
Zingiber officinale

*Fresh ginger is an important part of Chinese cuisine,
but it can also be used to add flavor to
savory dishes, especially meat.*

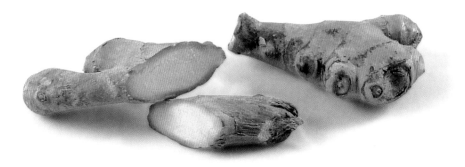

Undoubtedly one of the world's best-known spices, ginger was first mentioned in Chinese herbal medicine 2,000 years ago. It was used throughout Europe in medieval times to flavor meat dishes but it fell out of favor in the eighteenth century when the spice wars made it expensive. The flavor is warm, biting, sweet, and woody. Ginger tea is said to settle the stomach and ease morning sickness.

Description and parts used

Ginger is a perennial native to tropical Asia, although now cultivated in other tropical areas, especially Jamaica. It is the thick, fibrous root of *Z. officinale*, which grows to around 3 ft., with long spikes of flowers that are white or yellow with purple streaks.

The young rhizomes of the plant are used for fresh ginger and preserved, candied stem ginger, while dried ginger tends to come from older, more pungent rhizomes.

❦ CULINARY USES ❦

In Europe and North America, ginger is used to flavor desserts, cookies, and cakes (see recipe opposite), and is much loved as a flavoring for soft drinks. It is used all over Asia in appetizers and entrées, such as curries, salads, and relishes. In China, it features in many meat and vegetable stir-fries, and in Japan, it is pickled to make *beni shoga*, or it can be grated and used raw on tofu or noodles. The flowers of the plant are used in southeast Asian cuisine.

Fresh gingerroot should be peeled before it is cut into thin strips, or shredded and added to cooking. Dried ginger is the unpeeled root that has been dried and then ground to form powdered ginger. Ground ginger loses its flavor quickly, and it is best bought as dried root for grinding at home.

GINGER CAKE

This marvelous, spicy cake packed with ginger and syrup can be served with
a spoonful of heavy cream for extra luxury. Serves 12.

INGREDIENTS

Generous ¹/₃ cup molasses
Generous ¹/₃ cup corn syrup
Generous ¹/₂ cup dark brown sugar
¹/₄ lb butter
²/₃ cup whole milk
2¹/₄ cups self-rising flour
¹/₂ tsp salt
2 tsp ground ginger
2 oz preserved ginger in syrup, fine chopped

METHOD

1 Preheat the oven to 350°F. Grease and line an
   8 in. square cake pan.
2 Place the molasses, syrup, sugar, butter, and
   milk in a saucepan, and heat gently, stirring,
   until melted together.
3 Sift the flour, salt, and ground ginger in a
   bowl, and make a well in the center. Add
   the chopped ginger and gradually stir in the
   melted ingredients until well mixed.
4 Transfer to the prepared pan and bake in the
   center of the oven for about 75 minutes until
   well raised and firm to the touch. Allow to
   cool in the pan, then remove from the pan,
   wrap, and store for 24 hours. Cut into 12
   portions to serve.

HERB AND SPICE BLENDS

FIVE-SPICE POWDER

A famous Chinese spice blend, giving an aromatic and spicy touch to meat dishes.

1 tbsp Szechuan peppercorns
1 tbsp fennel seeds
3 star anise
1 small piece cinnamon
1 tsp cloves

1 Simply grind all the spices together to form a powder.
2 Store in an airtight container for up to 3 months.

FRENCH QUATRE ÉPICES (FOUR-SPICE)

A traditional French spice mixture that is used with cold meats and as a general spice blend for seasoning; it is quite hot.

1 tsp ground ginger
1 tsp ground cloves
1 tsp ground nutmeg
6 tsp ground white pepper

1 Mix all the ingredients together.
2 Store in an airtight container for up to 3 months.

BOUQUET GARNI

A selection of aromatic herbs used to flavor broths, soups, and casseroles. They usually include parsley, thyme, rosemary, and a bay leaf; celery leaf and leek are frequently added if available. They are tied together in a bundle with string (or wrapped in muslin) so that they don't separate in the dish, and they are discarded before serving.

CAJUN SEASONING

A piquant blend, popular in the southern states of the US.

2 tsp paprika
2 tsp dried garlic powder
2 tsp dried onion powder
$1/2$ tsp salt
$1/2$ tsp ground cumin
$1/2$ tsp cayenne pepper
$1/2$ tsp ground black pepper
1 tsp dried thyme

1 Mix all the ingredients together.
2 Store in an airtight container for up to 3 months.

PICKLING SPICE

A great combination of spices to use when there is a surplus of summer vegetables.

2 tbsp yellow mustard seeds
10 small dried red chilies
2 tbsp black peppercorns
2 tbsp allspice
1 tbsp cloves
1 small piece dried gingerroot, coarsely shredded

1 Tie the spices in a small, clean square of cheesecloth and add to the recipe as instructed—usually when making chutney.
2 Alternatively, add the spices directly to the pickling liquid for pickled vegetables and spiced vinegars.

FIVE-SPICE POWDER

FRENCH QUATRE ÉPICES

GARAM MASALA

GARAM MASALA

A potent mix that is highly spiced. Add in very small quantities toward the end of cooking.

2 tsp ground cinnamon
2$\frac{1}{2}$ tsp ground cloves
2 tsp ground bay leaves
2$\frac{1}{2}$ tsp ground cumin
1 tbsp ground black pepper
1$\frac{1}{2}$ tsp ground mace
1$\frac{1}{2}$ tsp ground cardamom

1 Mix all the ingredients together.
2 Store in an airtight container for up to
   3 months.

MILD CURRY POWDER

A gentle curry powder, formulated to please children and all those not used to hot curries.

1 tsp ground cardamom
1 tsp chili powder
1 tsp ground black pepper
1 tsp ground cumin
4 tsp ground coriander
1$\frac{1}{2}$ tsp ground turmeric
1 tsp ground fenugreek

1 Mix all the ingredients together.
2 Store in an airtight container for up to
   3 months.

HOT CURRY POWDER

For those who like their curry with plenty of heat. The amount of chili you use can vary according to your taste.

1 tsp cloves
2 tsp cardamom pods
1 tsp mustard seeds, dry roasted
1 tsp black poppy seeds
2 tsp chili powder
2 tsp ground cinnamon
2$\frac{1}{2}$ tsp ground cumin
$\frac{1}{2}$ tsp ground fenugreek
1 tsp ground nutmeg
2 tsp ground black pepper
1 tsp ground dried curry leaf

1 Grind the whole spices and seeds and mix
   with the ground spices and curry leaf.
2 Store in an airtight container for up to
   3 months.

MEDIUM CURRY PASTE

A spicy mix giving the authentic taste of India, without blasting your taste buds.

1$\frac{1}{2}$ tsp cumin seeds	1$\frac{1}{2}$ tsp chili powder
1$\frac{1}{2}$ tsp coriander	Pinch of salt
seeds	1 tsp dried mint
1 tsp garam masala	1 tbsp water
(see above)	1 tbsp lemon juice
1 tsp garlic powder	2 tbsp wine vinegar
$\frac{1}{2}$ tsp paprika	2 tbsp vegetable oil
1 tsp turmeric	

1 Grind the seeds and mix with the ground
   spices, salt, and mint. Stir well, add the water,
   lemon juice, and vinegar and mix to a paste.
2 Heat the oil slowly in a heavy skillet and stir in
   the paste. Cook gently for about 10 minutes,
   until all the water has been absorbed.
3 You can then use this paste as is.
   Alternatively, allow it to cool and store in an
   airtight glass jar, covered by a thin layer of oil,
   to keep it fresh for up to 2 weeks.

BIBLIOGRAPHY

A Dash of Spice
Kathryn Hawkins and Gail Duff
Reader's Digest, 1997

The Herbal Companion
Marcus A. Webb
People's Medical Society, 1997

The RHS Encyclopaedia of Herbs and Their Uses,
Deni Bown
Dorling Kindersley, 1995

The Complete Book of Herbs
Lesley Bremness
The National Trust, 1990

The Complete Book of Spices
Norman Gill
Dorling Kindersley, 1990

The Spice Companion
Richard Craze
Apple Press, 1997

The Complete Book of Herbs and Spices
Sarah Garland
Francis Lincoln, 1979

USEFUL ADDRESSES

AUSTRALIA
Spice Association of Australia
PO Box 104
St Leonards
NSW 2065, Australia

Australian Herb Society
PO Box 110
Mapleton
Queensland 4560, Australia

CANADA
National Herb and Spice Coalition
(NHSC)—national herb and spice directory
c/o SHSA
Box 18 Phippen
Saskatchewan, SOK 3E0, Canada
www.nationalherbspice.com

UK
Bart Spices—
herb and spice products, recipes, advice
York Road, Bedminster
Bristol, BS3 4AD, UK
www.bartspices.com

Fox's Spices
www.foxsspices.com—recipes, advice, suppliers

Herb Society—membership, nurseries and
suppliers, events, historic library
Sulgrave Manor, Sulgrave
Banbury, OX17 2SD, UK
www.herbsociety.co.uk

Redmoor
www.redmoor.net—mail order herbs and spices

Schwartz McCormick—herb and spice
products, recipes, advice
Thame Road, Haddenham
Buckinghamshire, HP17 8LB, UK
www.schwartz.co.uk

Spice World UK—mail order herbs, spices,
natural herb teas, and aromatherapy oils
Unit 6
New Forest Enterprise Centre
Rushington Business Park, Totton
Hampshire, SO40 9LA, UK
www.spiceworld.co.uk

USA
American Herb Association—
membership and advice
PO Box 1673
Nevada City, CA 9595
www.ahaherb.com

All American Spices
www.aaspices.bigstep.com—
herb and spice products and advice

American Spice Trade Association—
membership, links
2025 M Street, NW
Suite 800
Washington, DC 20036
www.astaspice.org

Herb Growing and Marketing Network—
membership, links
PO Box 245
Silver Spring, PA 17575-0245
www.herbworld.com

Herb Society of America—
membership, advice, promotion
9019 Kirtland, Chardon Road
Kirtland OH 44094
www.herbsociety.org

International Herb Association—
membership, links
P.O. Box 5667
Jacksonville, FL 32247-5667
www.iherb.org

INDEX